STEPHEN CRANE

HBJ ALBUM BIOGRAPHIES
EDITED BY MATTHEW J. BRUCCOLI

ROSS MACDONALD *by Matthew J. Bruccoli*
JACK KEROUAC *by Tom Clark*
JAMES JONES *by George Garrett*
STEPHEN CRANE *by James B. Colvert*

STEPHEN CRANE

BY

JAMES B. COLVERT

Harcourt Brace Jovanovich, Publishers · *San Diego   New York   London*

HBJ

Copyright © 1984 by James B. Colvert
All rights reserved. No part of this publication may be
reproduced or transmitted in any form or by any means,
electronic or mechanical, including photocopy, recording,
or any information storage and retrieval system, without
permission in writing from the publisher.

Requests for permission to make copies of any part of the work should be mailed to:
Permissions, Harcourt Brace Jovanovich, Publishers,
Orlando, FL 32887.

Photographs credited to Yale University are from the Collection of American Literature,
Beinecke Rare Book & Manuscript Library, Yale University.
Photographs credited to the Barrett Collection, University of Virginia, are from
the Stephen Crane Collection, Clifton Waller Barrett Library,
University of Virginia Library.
Photographs credited to Syracuse University are from
the George Arents Research Library
for Special Collections at Syracuse University.

Library of Congress Cataloging in Publication Data
Colvert, James B.
Stephen Crane.
(HBJ album biographies)
Bibliography: p.
Includes index.
1. Crane, Stephen, 1871–1900—Biography. 2. Novelists,
American—19th century—Biography. I. Title. II. Series.
PS1449.C85Z579 1984   813'.4 [B]   84–3805
ISBN 0–15–184958–7
ISBN 0–15–684946–1 (pbk.)

Designed by Joy Chu
Printed in the United States of America
First edition
A B C D E

FOR MARY

CONTENTS

ACKNOWLEDGMENTS

I AM INDEBTED to Professor Coburn Freer, Head of the Department of English, University of Georgia, for assisting me in my study of Stephen Crane by providing summer research funds. I am indebted also to a number of librarians for their valuable assistance in locating photographs of Crane and his associates: Mr. Gregory Johnson, Alderman Library, University of Virginia; Mr. Ronald Robbins, David Bishop Skillman Library, Lafayette College; Ms. Carolyn A. Davis, George Arents Research Library, Syracuse University; Mr. Stephen C. Jones, Beinecke Rare Book and Manuscript Library, Yale University; and Mr. Kenneth Lohf, Butler Library, Columbia University.

This sketch of Crane's life is grounded on the work of many scholars, but the writings of professors Fredson Bowers, J. C. Levenson, and Edwin Cady in the University Press of Virginia edition of *The Works of Stephen Crane* were indispensable in determining the order of certain events in Crane's history and the chronology of his works. I wish to thank Professor

Joseph Katz for his gift of a copy of Frederic M. Lawrence's valuable memoir of Crane. Professor Thomas Gullason's meticulous studies of Crane's early years were especially helpful in establishing the events and chronology of this shadowy period of his life.

I wish to express my particular appreciation to Barbara Colvert, who patiently read and typed the manuscript more than once and made many valuable suggestions for improving it.

CHRONOLOGY

1871   Stephen Crane, fourteenth and last child of the Reverend Jonathan Townley Crane, D. D., and Mary Helen Peck Crane, is born November 1 in Newark, New Jersey.

1878   Dr. Crane moves to Port Jervis, New York, to become pastor of the Drew Methodist Church. Stephen starts school.

1880   Dr. Crane dies on February 16.

1883   Mrs. Crane and Stephen move to Asbury Park, New Jersey. Stephen attends school where his sister Agnes is a teacher.

1885   Stephen writes his first story, "Uncle Jake and the Bell-Handle." Enrolls in the fall at Pennington Seminary, near Trenton.

1888   Enrolls at Claverack College and Hudson River Institute. Begins his career as a newspaper reporter gathering resort news along the Jersey coast for his brother Townley's news agency. His earliest published writings appear in Townley's *New York Tribune* column, "On the Jersey Coast."

1890   Enrolls at Lafayette College in mining engineering. Attends few classes and withdraws at the end of the first term on the advice of the dean.

1891   Enrolls in January as a special student at Syracuse University. Writes articles for the *New York Tribune*, publishes his first story, "The King's Favor," in the *University Herald*, and acquires a local reputation as a baseball player. Meets Hamlin Garland, whose lectures on American literature he attends in August at Avon-by-the-Sea, New Jersey.

1892   Five of his Sullivan County sketches appear in Sunday editions of the *Tribune* in July. Dismissed by the *Tribune* in August when his ironic account of a parade of workers in Asbury Park proves politically embarrassing to Whitelaw Reid, owner of the paper and candidate for Vice President of the United States. Moves to New York in the fall to work for the *Herald*. Begins a novel about a prostitute, *Maggie: A Girl of the Streets*.

1893   Unable to find a publisher for his novel, pays a New York job printer to produce 1,100 copies. *Maggie* appears in March under the pseudonym Johnston Smith. The novel wins him the friendship of Garland and William Dean Howells, chief literary realists of the day. Begins a draft of *The Red Badge of Courage* in April.

1894   Begins another New York novel, *George's Mother*, in the spring. A severely shortened version of *The Red Badge of Courage* appears in the *Philadelphia Press* and other newspapers in December.

1895   Begins a tour of the West and Mexico as a roving reporter for the Bacheller-Johnson Syndicate. Meets Willa Cather in Lincoln,

Nebraska. Appleton accepts *The Red Badge of Courage* for book publication. His first volume of poems, *The Black Riders*, appears in May. Returns from Mexico and settles at Hartwood, New York, a village near Port Jervis. In the fall begins the stories for *The Little Regiment* and a novel, *The Third Violet*. *The Red Badge of Courage* is published in book form in October.

1896   Between January and June becomes famous at home and abroad as the author of *The Red Badge of Courage*. Discovered in England by Joseph Conrad, H. G. Wells, and Harold Frederic. Incurs the enmity of the New York police when he testifies on behalf of Dora Clark, a prostitute who charges a police officer with false arrest. Leaves New York in November to report the Cuban insurrection against Spain for the Bacheller Syndicate.

1897   In Jacksonville, Florida, meets Cora Stewart, proprietress of a discreet bordello, the Hotel de Dream. Survives the sinking of the "filibuster" ship *Commodore* off the coast of Florida on January 2. Writes "The Open Boat" before leaving Florida, accompanied by Cora, to report the Greco-Turkish war for the *New York Journal*. After the war, settles in England with Cora. Warmly received by Ford Madox Hueffer (later Ford), Edward Garnett, and Henry James. Writes "The Bride Comes to Yellow Sky," "Death and the Child," *The Monster*, and other stories.

1898   Writes "The Blue Hotel." Returns to the United States in April to report the Spanish-American war for the *New York World*. A collection of stories, *The Open Boat and Other Tales of Adventure*, appears the same month. Begins *Active Service*, a novel based on his Greek adventures.

1899   Returns to England in January. Though beset by money problems, takes up residence with Cora and a large retinue of servants at Brede Place, an ancient English manor near Hastings in southern England. Continues his friendships with Conrad, Wells, Hueffer, and James. Publishes a second volume of poems, *War Is Kind*, and the novel *Active Service*, and begins, under the burdens of failing health and increasing debts, a fanciful Irish romance, *The O'Ruddy*. Suffering from tuberculosis and complications resulting from malaria contracted in Cuba, he collapses in December with severe hemorrhaging of the lungs.

1900   Works intermittently on *The O'Ruddy*, publishes *Wounds in the Rain*, a volume of Cuban war stories, and *Whilomville Stories*, a collection of tales based on his adventures as a child in Port Jervis. Writes some of the pieces that appeared in *Last Words* in 1902 and works on the novel *The O'Ruddy* (finished by Robert Barr and published in 1903). When the attacks grow more severe in the spring, Cora takes him to a sanitarium in Badenweiler, Germany, where he dies on June 5.

INTRODUCTION

STEPHEN CRANE'S short and brilliant literary career began in the summer of 1892 when the *New York Tribune* printed five anecdotal little stories based on his camping and fishing adventures in Sullivan County, New York. It ended eight years later when he died in Badenweiler, Germany, from tuberculosis and the effects of his strenuous and reckless life as a war correspondent. When he died, five months short of his twenty-ninth birthday, he left, besides his voluminous journalistic work, a half-dozen novels, two books of poems, and more than a hundred stories, sketches, and miscellaneous writings, enough altogether to fill ten large volumes in the University of Virginia edition of his works. Some of these writings brought him high fame in his own lifetime and eventually established him, after more than two decades of neglect, as a major figure in the history of American literature, a pioneer experimenter in forms and styles which profoundly influenced the new fiction of the 1920s.

Crane was indisputably the most gifted American writer of his generation, and the most precocious. He wrote his first novel, *Maggie: A Girl of the Streets* (1893), when he was only twenty-one, and his masterpiece, *The Red Badge of Courage* (1895), when he was twenty-three. Both were boldly unconventional, notable for their innovative impressionistic style, vivid irony, and penetrating psychological realism—all characteristics of style and vision that anticipated Hemingway, Fitzgerald, Anderson, and Faulkner by twenty-five years. His fame declined suddenly and sharply after his death, and for more than two decades he was all but forgotten, except by a few literary men like Joseph Conrad, H. G. Wells, Edward Garnett, and Ford Madox Ford. These men, his friends and neighbors during his sojourn in England in the last years of his life, grasped fully the significance of his work. "Your method is fascinating," Conrad wrote him shortly after their first meeting in 1897. "You are a complete impressionist."[1] Garnett, an unusually perceptive critic, described Crane's unique art and its powers with precision and insight in 1898 in an essay published just as Crane was returning to England from his ordeal as a war correspondent in Cuba.

But it was H. G. Wells, in a piece written a few weeks after Crane's death, who predicted with uncanny accuracy his significance for the literary future. To Wells his work represented a turning point in the history of imaginative writing. Crane, he observed, broke sharply with established conventions and pointed the way to the methods and attitudes of a new era. His rejection of the past, particularly the innocent pieties and assumptions of his personal religious heritage, was so radical that it seemed to Wells that "racial thought and tradition had been razed from his mind and its site plowed and salted." In style and method, the critic wrote, "he is sharply defined, the expression in literary art of certain enormous repudiations." He eliminated "obviously and sedulously" most of the familiar devices of the nineteenth-century literary prose style, dispensing with such artifices as "richness of allusion, any melody or balance of phrase, the half quotation that refracts and softens and enriches the statement, the momentary digression that opens like a window upon beautiful or distant things. . . ." As a link between the nineteenth and twentieth centuries, Wells prophesied, he "will be found to occupy a position singularly cardinal" as "the first expression of the opening mind of a new period."[2]

Though remembered by these men and by literary memoirists who occasionally made him the subject of casual anecdotes, Crane rested in near obscurity for the next twenty years. "I hardly meet anyone now who knows or remembers anything of him," Conrad wrote bitterly in 1912.[3] A character in Wells's *Boon* (1915), undoubtedly speaking for the author, says, "America can produce such a supreme writer as Stephen Crane—the best writer of English for the last half century. . . . But America won't own such children. . . . She'll sit never knowing she's had a Stephen Crane."[4] But signs of a rediscovery appeared in the early twenties. Garnett's superb essay in *Friday Nights* (1922) focused once again on the essential issues of Crane's vision and style: his unique quality, the critic wrote in a passage that recent writers have built on elaborately, was "his wonderful insight into, and mastery of the primary passions, and his irony deriding the swelling emotions of the self. It is his irony that checks the emotional intensity of his delineation, and suddenly reveals passion at high tension in the clutch of the implacable tides of life. It is the perfect fusion of these two forces of passion and irony that creates Crane's spiritual background, and raises his work, at its finest, into the higher zone of man's tragic conflict with the universe."[5]

All his work, except *The Red Badge of Courage*, was out of print until 1921, when Vincent Starrett brought out a selection of stories under the title *Men, Women, and Boats*. Thomas Beer published a colorful, impressionistic biography of Crane in 1923, and Wilson Follett edited his collected work in twelve volumes in the mid-twenties. Amy Lowell, Willa Cather, Sherwood Anderson, Joseph Hergesheimer, and H. L. Mencken helped in their appreciative introductions to these volumes to focus attention on Crane once more, recognizing in his experiments with new subjects, themes, and forms something of the spirit of their own literary views and aims. Mencken noted that *The Red Badge*, "at once unprecedented and irresistible," gave the literary nineties "a sudden direction and a powerful impulse forward," away from the genteel realism of William Dean Howells and his imitators "with its puerile labouring of trivialities." Crane's was a "sterner, more searching realism that got under the surface. . . ."[6] Like other writers of the twenties, Anderson, who said Crane was an "explosion," felt at home with his indifference to conventional plot, his preoccupation with the drama of thought and feeling in the mental life of his subjects, his daring metaphorical treatment of psychological events, and his vivid sense of unfolding experience as a gradual revelation of ultimate mysteries. A relativist, ironist, and impressionist, Crane seemed to these writers to belong more to their own time than to the nineties.

Literary historians, particularly those who wrote the official academic histories, were not so sympathetic, then or later. Ignoring the implications of Crane's radical style, they were inclined to view him either as a perfervid journalist or, at best, an imitator of the "morbid" French naturalists, especially of Zola, and to measure him conservatively by the conventions of nineteenth-century documentary realism. A standard history of American fiction in 1936 found his insignificance in his preoccupation with the ugliness of violence and squalor,[7] and Fred Lewis Pattee, responding in 1939 to the publisher Alfred Knopf's request for advice about bringing out a volume of Crane's stories, replied that Crane "was not a short story writer at all" but a "forced growth . . . of modern journalism," a "mere newspaper camera set up for movie use or for the daily journal column, alive today; tomorrow in the ash barrel."[8]

Since the early 1950s, when John Berryman's lively biography and R. W. Stallman's anthology of Crane's best writings appeared, he has been the focus of intense scholarly and critical study. Hundreds of essays and a full score of books have been written about him; a new and exhaustively complete edition of his works in ten volumes was issued by the University Press of Virginia in the late sixties and seventies. Crane is now universally acknowledged as one of the most original of our writers and has been accorded at last the place in literary history Wells predicted for him long ago. The story of his life—as it leads from his earliest days in a Methodist parsonage to the resort beaches of Asbury Park, into the infamous Bowery and foul slums of New York, through the rugged country of the West and Mexico, to Florida and the disaster of shipwreck, and to the battlefields of Greece and Cuba—reveals the experiences his imagination transmuted into an art that expresses a compelling vision of life and marks him unmistakably as a major force in modern literature.

STEPHEN CRANE

ONE

THE PARSONAGE

STEPHEN CRANE was born November 1, 1871, at 14 Mulberry Street, Newark, New Jersey, the fourteenth and last child of the Reverend Jonathan Townley Crane, D.D., and Mary Helen Peck Crane. Noting the event in his journal, Dr. Crane proudly explained the significance of his new son's Christian name: "We call him Stephen, the name of the ancestor of the Elizabethtown Cranes, who was one of the Company of 'Associates' who settled at E. town in 1665; also of S. Crane of Revolutionary times, who was prominent in patriotic labors and counsels for 15 years."[1] The first Stephen, one of the sixty-five settlers who joined Governor Philip Carteret in 1665 in founding Elizabethtown, was prominent in the affairs of the new community. He led a minor rebellion against the governor when this none-too-scrupulous official illegally granted a town lot to a political favorite.

The second Stephen, the patriot of Revolutionary days, was the grandson of the Elizabethtown Stephen, and as Dr. Crane noted, played a distinguished role indeed in the early history of New Jersey. He was sheriff of Essex County under George III, judge of the Court of Common Pleas during the agitation over the Stamp Act, Speaker of the New Jersey House of Representatives, and a two-term member of the First Continental Congress. He was in Philadelphia at the time of the Declaration of Independence and would have been one of the signers (as Dr. Crane mistakenly thought he was) if he had not been called home two weeks before its adoption to help quell noisy Tories in the state legislature. "I am not much on this sort of thing," Stephen wrote much later in a sketch of this famous ancestor's honors and achievements, "or I could write more, but at any rate the family is founded deep in Jersey soil . . . and I am about as much of a Jerseyman as you can find."[2] Once during a visit to Philadelphia Crane dragged a friend down to Carpenter's Hall to show him this venerable old Stephen's portrait in a painting of the First Continental Congress; "and strange to say," the friend reported, "in the profile there was a striking likeness."[3]

William, the patriot's oldest son, was a colonel in command of the Sixth Regiment of New Jersey Infantry during the Revolution and was wounded in the expedition of Quebec. The patriot's youngest son died a hero's death in the Revolution. Captured by a band of Hessians near Elizabethtown, he refused to answer questions about his regiment, which the Hessians planned to attack, and they beat and stabbed him and left him dead in the road. Colonel Crane's son, also named William, was a distinguished naval commander during the War of 1812, and was cited for bravery as captain of the brig *Vixen* in attacks against Tripoli and the Barbary pirates in 1815.

These illustrious forebears made a deep impression on Crane and figured significantly in shaping his imagination. Their courage and devotion to duty came to represent for him the virtues of the true aristocrat, the man who stands firmly to his duty, regardless of risk, in times of supreme crisis. Toward the end of his life he worked briefly on a plan for a novel about the Revolution in New Jersey, in which Stephen Crane the patriot and Colonel William were to be principal characters. "I swear by the real aristocrat," he wrote. "The man whose forefathers were men of courage, sympathy and wisdom is usually one who will stand the strain whatever it may be. He is like a thorough-bred horse. His nerves may be high and he will do a lot of jumping often but in the crises he settles down and becomes the most reliable and enduring of created things."[4] The idea surfaces regularly in his writings.

Crane's father, born in 1819 near Elizabeth, was brought up a Presbyterian; but that stern theology, especially the doctrine of infant damnation, did not appeal to his gentle, hopeful nature, and when he was about eighteen he was converted at a revival meeting to the Methodist Episcopal Church. Graduating from the College of New Jersey (Princeton College) in 1843, he began the next year his long and arduous career as preacher, educator, and religious writer. In 1849 he became principal of Pennington Seminary, near Trenton, which within a few years he had made into one of the leading preparatory schools in the state. Dickinson College awarded him the degree of Doctor of Divinity in 1856.

He wrote several books on Methodist codes of conduct and doctrine, one of which—*Holiness, the Birthright of All God's Children* (1874)—was admired by his colleagues for the vigor and clarity of its analysis of certain abstruse theological questions. In *Popular Amusements* (1869) he warned against the destructive effects of dancing, trashy novels, cards, smoking, and drinking; and in *Arts of Intoxication* (1870), a leading temperance text in its day, he resolved a contradiction between Scripture and the almost equally sacred principle of total abstinence by theorizing that Noah's drunkenness was unintentional. "Very possibly," he wrote, "the process of fermentation had not before been noticed, the results were not known, and the consequences in this case were wholly unexpected."[5] Stephen was to remember him for his gentleness and innocence. "He was so simple and good," he once said, "that I often think he didn't know much of anything about humanity."[6] In an old engraving he appears as a mild-looking, bearded patriarch, gazing benevolently and bemusedly from behind thick school masterish spectacles.

Crane's mother, Mary Helen, was also a dedicated Methodist, the only daughter of the Reverend George Peck, D.D., of Wilkes-Barre, Pennsylvania, and descendant of a long line of preachers extending back to frontier days. In that family, Crane once wrote, "everybody as soon as he could walk, became a Methodist clergyman—of the old ambling-nag, saddle-bag, exhorting kind."[7] Dr. Peck was an important figure in the church, prominent as a writer and as editor of the *Methodist Quarterly Review*, to which Dr. Crane was a regular contributor, and an authority on doctrine and policy. His four brothers were also Methodist ministers, and one was the venerable Reverend Jesse Peck, D.D., LL.D., a bishop and one of the founders of Syracuse University. He was the author of a forbidding treatise on sin, *What Must I Do to Be Saved?* (1858), a memorable hellfire-and-brimstone warning to sinners of the wrath of a jealous and vengeful God. His grandnephew Stephen inherited his father's copy of this book, which became an important influence on his quizzical poems about God in *The Black Riders* and, as a focal point of his intellectual rebellion, a significant, though oblique, influence on most of his other writings.

After her marriage to young Jonathan Crane in 1848, Mary Helen became active in missionary and reform work, and by the mid-eighties was prominent in the New Jersey temperance movement. As state superintendent of press for the Women's Christian Temperance Union, she was much in demand as a speaker and appeared frequently before the New Jersey legislature and various reform organizations to attack such evils as alcohol, gambling, and prizefighting. She also wrote articles on religion and reform for the *New York Tribune* and the New York Associated Press, and every August went to Ocean Grove, "the Mecca of the Methodists" on the Jersey coast near Asbury Park, to report the great religious and temperance conferences—"the Methodist holy show," Crane called it. "She was always starting off when she felt well enough to some big prayer meeting or experience meeting," he wrote, "and she spoke very well. . . . She spoke as slowly as a big clock ticks and her effects were impromptu."[8] As firm in her religious beliefs as her father and uncles, she was also generous and sympathetic. "My mother was a very religious woman," her son said, "but I don't think that she was as narrow as most of her friends or her family."[9] She once defied community standards of respectability by taking an unwed mother and her baby into the Crane home. "Inopportune babies are not part of Methodist ritual," he wrote, "but mother was always more of a Christian than a Methodist and she kept this girl at our house . . . until she found a home somewhere."[10]

But she was inflexible in her religious convictions. One of her nieces wrote that Stephen as a young man "did marvel always that such an intellectual woman . . . capable of being a regular contributor to magazines and newspapers, could have wrapped herself so completely in the 'vacuous, futile, psalm-singing that passed for worship' in those days."[11] In a photograph taken in the 1880s she appears as a homely, worn, fragile-looking woman, but the firm set of her mouth and bold gaze suggest uncommon will and determination. Her piety and simple orthodoxy Crane depicted with ambivalent tenderness and irony in the doting and deluded Mrs. Kelcey in his novel *George's Mother*.

Though Stephen had six surviving brothers and two sisters, they were so much older than he that his position in the family was much like that of an only child. When he was born, the youngest of his brothers, Luther, was eight, and the oldest, George, was twenty-one. Of the two girls, the younger, Agnes, was fifteen; Mary Helen, the oldest of the children, was twenty-two. Two of the boys, William, seventeen, and Townley, Jr., nineteen, were to play important roles in his future, but in his earliest years it was Agnes who influenced him most, even more in some ways than his busy, middle-aged parents (Dr. Crane was fifty-two, Mrs. Crane forty-five when he was born). Plain, gifted, temperamental, Agnes was Stephen's surrogate mother, taking him in charge when Mrs. Crane was away, as she often was, at religious or reform meetings. Agnes was literary: she aspired to be a novelist, despite her father's view that fiction was more often than not mere idle amusement, and sinful if it did not point a clear moral. She wanted first, as she said, "to be a Christian lady" and then "to *write*."[12] She lavished attention and affection on her small brother, nursed him in his frequent sicknesses, directed his reading, and supervised his first efforts at writing little stories and poems. This small alliance, formed in the spirit of Agnes's independence and mild, ladylike rebelliousness, was undoubtedly the remotest source of those "enormous repudiations" H. G. Wells cited years later as the primary motives of Crane's life and art.

Dr. Crane was Presiding Elder, or chief administrative officer, of the Newark and Elizabeth Conferences until 1876, when he was appointed pastor of the Cross Street Church in Paterson. Two years later he moved to Port Jervis, New York, where he became pastor of the Drew Methodist Church in the spring of 1878. Situated in the low hills of southwestern New York, Port Jervis was the archetypal rural village of that era of American innocence and simplicity. Main Street, which had no stores or commercial buildings in 1878, curved around broad-porched houses and spreading lawns past the high, sharp steeple of Dr. Crane's church. In the valleys below were resort hotels; to the north, stretching toward the distant Catskills, was the wilderness of Sullivan County, that "country of elastic miles flowing over hills and rocks and around lakes and through hemlock woods"[13] which Crane came to know intimately as camper, hunter, and

Crane's mother, Mary Helen Peck Crane, probably taken about 1889

Stephen Crane at age two (courtesy Syracuse University)

fisherman in the eighties and nineties. Port Jervis became the model for the village in *The Third Violet* and the fictional Whilomville in the late tales of childhood in the *Whilomville Stories.* The Sullivan County wilderness was the model for the ambiguously sinister and pastoral landscape of his earliest fiction, the Sullivan County sketches, as well as of *The Red Badge of Courage* and other writings.

In the fall of 1879 he started to school and, having the advantage of Agnes's devoted coaching, made impressive progress. "They tell me that I got through two grades in six weeks," he said later, "which sounds like the lie of a fond mother at a tea party but I do remember that I got ahead very fast and that father was pleased with me."[14] Sometimes Dr. Crane took him along when he drove out in his buggy to communities near Port Jervis to preach or conduct funerals, and little incidents stuck in his memory, especially those which revealed his father's gentle unworldiness. "Once we got mixed up in an Irish funeral near a place named Slate Hill. Everybody was drunk and father was scandalized." Once in Middletown, while his father was engaged at the church, Stephen wandered into a pasture and tried to shoot a cow with a toy gun his brother William had given him. The incident upset Dr. Crane "wonderfully" and gave Stephen the germ for one of his Whilomville stories, "Lynx-Hunting." His gentle father was fond of animals, he recalled, "and never drove a horse faster than two yards an hour even if some Christian was dying elsewhere."[15] His youngest son inherited this kindly trait.

Agnes, who graduated from Centenary Collegiate Institute at Hackettstown as class valedictorian in 1880 and began teaching school at Port Jervis in 1881 or 1882, continued to encourage his childish literary efforts. "I remember when I was eight years old," he wrote, "I became very much interested in a child character called, I think, Little Goodie Brighteyes, and I wrote a story then which I called after this fascinating little person."[16] The title suggests that it might have been something like the pious fables Dr. Crane wrote in 1873 for the *Sunday-School Classmate*, in which he celebrated the beauty and harmony of God's nature, the dire consequences of cheating in school, and the moral repugnance of cruelty to cats and dogs. But "Little Goodie Brighteyes" has not survived, and the only example of Stephen's literary experiments from these earliest years is a four-stanza poem, written when he was eight or nine and preserved by Agnes, which celebrates precociously the superiority of dogs over sweaters, wool suits, and bicycles as Christmas gifts:

Crane as a boy of five or six (courtesy Barrett Collection, University of Virginia)

Last Christmas they gave me a sweater,
  And a nice warm suit of wool,
But I'd rather be cold and have a dog,
  To watch when I come from school.[17]

One bitter day in February of 1880, Dr. Crane died suddenly of heart failure, and the placid life of the parsonage, guarded by his high Christian idealism, came to a sudden end. In the first uncertain months after this unsettling loss, Mrs. Crane and Stephen lived in a boarding house in Rose-ville, near Newark. But Stephen was dangerously sick with scarlet fever there, and when he recovered they moved back to the healthier climate of Port Jervis. Agnes began teaching at the town school about this same time, and William, newly graduated from law school, set up practice there in 1882. Mrs. Crane, who Stephen said "lived in and for religion" after her husband's death, had become more deeply involved in church work than ever. In the spring of 1883, she moved to Asbury Park, a vacation town on the Jersey coast only a mile or so north of Ocean Grove, the Methodist center Dr. Crane had helped establish years before. Agnes, unhappy over problems with rowdy boys in her classes, resigned her teaching job at Port Jervis and took a position at the Asbury Park School, where Stephen (still a good student though no longer in the top rank) enrolled in the fall of 1883. Townley, his worldly, eccentric brother, now a newspaperman, owned and operated a news agency at Asbury Park. Known as "the shore fiend" for his relentless pursuit of trivial news items in the little beach communities along the coast, Townley supplied paragraphs to the *New York Tribune* and the Associated Press about arrivals and departures at the resort hotels, religious conferences at Ocean Grove, and the concerts and lectures at nearby Avon-by-the-Sea.

To Stephen, now eleven, Asbury Park was freedom. A "pale-faced, blond-headed, hungry-looking boy,"[18] as a childhood friend remembered him, he roamed the beaches, loitered around Townley's agency and the resort hotels, and played baseball and football with passionate intensity. After a time, it was said, no one in Asbury Park could throw a ball he could not catch bare-handed. When Agnes died in June of "cerebrospinal meninges," Stephen came under the more worldly influence of his brothers Townley and William, who had long ago put aside the religious disciplines and dogmas of their parents and now seemed willing enough to help

Stephen do the same. William, he recalled, used to try to argue with his mother about religion, "but he always gave it up. . . . You could argue just as well with a wave." Stephen was more receptive. "I used to like church and prayer meeting when I was a kid," he said, "but that cooled off and when I was thirteen or about that, my brother Will [William] told me not to believe in Hell after my uncle had been boring me about the lake of fire and the rest of the sideshows."[19]

Mrs. Crane worried about her sons, especially about her youngest, when they seemed to be giving up their belief in eternal damnation and salvation. "Stevie is like the wind in Scripture," she told friends. "He bloweth where he listeth." By 1885 he was flouting the rules of Methodists and Temperance Unionists alike. "Once when I was fourteen an organ grinder on the beach at Asbury gave me a nice long drink out of a nice red bottle for picking up his hat for him," he said. "I felt ecstatic walking home and then I was an Emperor and some Rajahs and Baron de Blowitz all at the same time. I had been sulky all morning and now I was perfectly willing to go to a prayer meeting and Mother was tickled to death. And, mind you, all because this nefarious Florentine gave me a red drink out of a bottle. I have frequently wondered how much mothers ever know about their sons, after all."[20] The sense of guilt and alienation obliquely acknowledged in this reminiscence is pervasive in *George's Mother*, which dramatizes the disastrous consequences of a willful young man's alcoholic revolt against his sentimentally pious mother.

As for Stephen's distressing apostasy, Pennington Seminary, which Dr. Crane had established many years before as a model of Methodist piety and discipline, would inevitably occur to Mrs. Crane as an ideal corrective. Located in the secluded village of Pennington some miles north of Trenton (removed from the temptations of town life, its catalogue pointed out), the seminary was still much alive to the memory of Dr. Crane. Many of the precepts he advocated in his books on Christian conduct were still evident in the school's policies and programs. In 1885, Crane's first year there, a Methodist report boasted of its "thorough work in study and teaching," its excellent discipline, and its "religious atmosphere . . . of an intense revival character."[21] When Mrs. Crane enrolled the fourteen-year-old Stephen there in September, she might well have felt that he was once again under the benign influence of his father.

The curriculum stressed language, literature, and history; there were also courses in etymology, grammar, and rhetoric, and English composition was required throughout the entire academic year. (Oddly, Stephen Crane never mastered certain elementary principles of grammar, punctuation, and spelling.) But the most formidable requirement for the indifferent Stephen was the routine religious observances: services twice daily in the school chapel, services Sunday mornings in one of the two churches in the village, Bible classes in the chapel Sunday afternoons, and general prayer meetings Wednesday evenings—a dramatic contrast to the freedom of the beaches at Asbury Park and the easy skepticism around Townley's news agency.

There was doubtless consolation in football and baseball, important sports at Pennington. There is no proof that he played either, but he was very likely on the baseball team, since he reported to Will and Mrs. Crane on one occasion that he had decided to be a professional baseball player. "But ma says it's not a serious occupation," he wrote a friend, "and Will says I have to go to college first."[22] It was probably Will, a student of the battles of Chancellorsville and Gettysburg, who first stirred his interest in war and perhaps told him about the illustrious deeds of his military ancestors. In any case, Stephen had been fascinated with war from his earliest childhood, and when his ambitions to be a baseball player were dampened, he turned his thoughts to a career in the army. Some time before the end of the winter term of 1887, he persuaded his mother to allow him to transfer to Claverack College and Hudson River Institute, a semimilitary, coeducational school near the tiny Dutch village of Claverack in the Hudson valley in central New York. He enrolled in January 1888, apparently with some vague notion of preparing for the entrance examinations to West Point.

Like Pennington Seminary, Claverack College was a Methodist school. It had once been one of the leading collegiate institutions in the state; but by the time Crane arrived, it had been all but absorbed by the Hudson River Institute, an undistinguished military boarding school patronized largely by parents burdened with doltish or intractable sons. Its discipline and standards had sharply declined. There was "a certain devilish, care-free spirit abroad," one of his classmates, Harvey Wickham, wrote. "Students . . . roamed as in a terrestrial paradise like packs of cheerful wolves out of bounds, out of hours and very much out of hand."[23] Its faculty of sixteen taught the usual courses in mathematics, science, languages, history, literature, composition, and elocution, but Crane was chiefly interested in baseball, military drill, poker, and girls. "I never learned anything there," he said once. "American private schools are not as bad as our public schools, perhaps, but there is no great difference. . . . But heaven was sunny blue and no rain fell on the diamond when I was playing baseball. I was very happy, there."[24]

He was an outstanding catcher and also a talented military drill-master. At the beginning of his second year he was corps adjutant and first lieutenant of the crack C Company, which won the coveted Washington's Birthday drill prize in 1890. He had "enough of the true officer in him," Wickham recalled, "to have a perfectly hen-like attitude toward the rank and file."[25] In the spring of 1890, he was elected captain of the baseball team, an honor he declined in favor of first baseman Jones, and was promoted to captain in the military corps. He was madly in love with Harriet Mattison, "our best pianist," Wickham recalled, noted for her skill in playing Schumann. After her untimely death, he was in love with Jennie Pierce, who made his life "miserable," as he said, "with only half an effort."[26] His friends were Earl Reeves, of Rushville, Indiana, whom Crane dubbed "the Rushville Indian" or "Sioux," and Odell Hathaway and other "tough devils" who hung around in Sioux's room for secret poker and cigarettes.

A photograph of Crane in his school uniform, made some time in his first year at Claverack, shows a handsome youth with well-shaped head, prominent bladed nose, full mouth, and large expressive eyes; his hair is fashionably parted on one side and trimmed in a kind of half bang which slants across the left side of his forehead. In the suggestion of a certain middle-class correctness there is no hint of another side of Crane. He was notoriously untidy, and unconventional in thought and expression. To boys like Wickham, who never penetrated his reserve, he seemed self-absorbed and arrogant. He swore, played poker, smoked, and drank beer—certain signs of wickedness in those days.

But his instinct for rebellion betrayed in these small defiances seemed to clash dramatically on occasion with his abiding commitment to the ethical values of his Methodist heritage. "Undoubtedly," Wickham wrote, "he felt himself peculiar, an oyster beneath whose lips there was already an irritating grain of some foreign substance."[27] He avoided Judd's notorious pie shop in Claverack where local Don Juans sometimes sat on dark stairs with certain girls, and he seldom went into Hudson, "our neighboring and

Crane as a lieutenant in the Hudson River Institute cadet corps,
1889 or 1890 (courtesy Barrett Collection, University of Virginia)

deliciously wicked city, where, according to rumor, initiation was to be had into the ultimate mysteries of life. . . ."[28] Wickham once overheard him say to a reputed seducer, "I hear you're bad—I hear you're damn bad."[29] And yet, as his classmate observed, "he enjoyed a certain reputation for villainy," probably because of the faculty's "nice instinct . . . for distinguishing veritable young Samsons from among the ordinary bad boys who merely scribble adolescent obscenities upon the temple walls."[30]

In any case, there was an unresolved tension in him between piety and sinfulness, authority and rebellion. An eloquent sentence in a piece he wrote for the school magazine, the *Vidette*, celebrating the first game of the 1890 baseball season, shows his first tentative exploration of the ironic implications of these conflicts: "The village dominie, who ordinarily is looked upon with awe and reverence, sinks gloomily behind the pall of favoritism on these occasions, and may be seen to complacently stand for more than an hour beside the worst boy of boarding school fame, and look admiringly upon his sin stained brow as he explains a new feature in the game."[31] This wry commentary on the ascendancy of the disreputable urchin over the revered minister, obviously derived from personal history, verifies the faculty's instinct: it is the sign of a rebelliousness more consequential indeed than poker and beer.

In the summer of 1888, his first year at Claverack, he started working for Townley as a cub reporter, gathering gossipy items from the resort hotels and the Methodist center at Ocean Grove for Townley's Sunday *Tribune* column, "On the Jersey Coast." He sometimes wrote parts of these columns himself, anonymous paragraphs, usually trivial enough, being mere notices of arrivals and departures, announcements of meetings, brief reviews of lectures, and the like. Occasionally, though, he ventured a tentative satirical note in the sly mockery of a turn of phrase, telling word, or odd juxtaposition, as in, for example, his paragraph praising a revivalist, the Reverend Yatman, for his ability to win souls "to higher things" when he conducted a "love feast" at Ocean Grove. Reverend Yatman, he wrote, earnestly requested a congregation of six thousand to "shake hands in token of brotherly love, which they did with shouts and tears," and four Chinamen "sent up a written testimony that they 'loved Jesus better and better every day.' "[32] His friends of this time remembered him as companionable and fun-loving. "He had a keen sense of the dramatic," one recalled, "and his countenance usually displayed an amused, satirical, but kindly grin. His keen mind instantly caught the absurd, bizarre, or ridiculous aspect of any incident, and he would draw out an account of it in his own entertaining fashion."[33] In February 1890, his first signed publication appeared in the *Vidette*. It was a bland class essay on Stanley's African expedition in search of Livingstone and celebrated such virtues in the explorer as his sacrificial devotion to duty and his stalwart Christian faith.

The admired Reverend General John B. Van Petten, professor of history and elocution and a distinguished veteran of the battles of Chancellorsville and Winchester, may have helped keep Crane's interest in war alive; but by the spring of 1890 Will had apparently persuaded him to give up his plan for a career in the army. A more practical profession, as his brother probably suggested, would be mining engineering, especially since the family owned stock in a Pennsylvania coal mine. So in the fall of 1890 he rode the train out to Easton, Pennsylvania, with what reluctance is not recorded, to register at Lafayette College as a freshman in mining engineering.

It would be hard to imagine a situation less congenial to a youth of Crane's temperament, interests, and gifts. In these years the curriculum at Lafayette was extraordinarily narrow, conservative, and conventional. Instruction was rigidly set in a pattern of mechanical class recitation, and mining engineering was notoriously uninspiring. Courses in the English department, largely philological, required no writing. Students wrote papers only for their professors in the departments of their special fields, and only on topics in those fields "in the words and phrases current among experts." Instruction, even in the sciences, was keyed to religious doctrine. "In addition to the systematic and thorough study of the Word of God in all classes," the college catalogue stated, "special attention will be given to the harmony of Science with Revealed Religion"; even the course in physiology in the Physical Culture department gave "special consideration . . . to the bearing of the facts and principles upon Natural Theology."[34]

Crane enrolled in courses in Milton, Bible, geometry, algebra, drawing, chemistry, and French, but he seldom attended classes in any of them. Although baseball season was still months in the future, he haunted the diamond, playing nearly every afternoon in pickup intramural games. Or he was in the local poolroom where he played bad pool with a youth who was struck by his daring and self-assured ideas about literature. Usually reticent in talking about books, a fact that had led some biographers to underestimate his reading, he was, as a classmate at Claverack reported, "a voracious" reader of nineteenth-century English literature and of the Greek and Roman classics. At Lafayette he talked to his poolroom companion about Tolstoy, whom he proclaimed the world's greatest writer (though he knew at that time, apparently, only one of his novels, *Sebastopol*); Flaubert's *Salammbô*, he declared, was too long, and Henry James's *The Reverberator* was a tedious bore. He never liked James's work much, though in the last year of his life he became the novelist's personal friend.

At the end of the semester he received grades in only four of his seven courses: 60 in algebra, 92 in elocution, 88 in French, and zero in theme writing. The cause of his failures, according to the clerk of the faculty, was poor class attendance. The dean probably advised him to withdraw, though Crane almost certainly had decided to do so on his own. "We all counted on him to make the baseball team in the spring," a contemporary wrote, "and he returned for a short period after the Christmas holidays. Then he packed up quietly and without saying much to anybody, aside from the fact . . . that his family affairs would not permit him to remain at Lafayette, he quietly took his departure."[35] Crane's comment on the first semester of his college career was succinct enough: "I went to Lafayette College but did not graduate. I found mining-engineering not at all to my taste. I preferred baseball."[36]

Still hopeful that a sound Methodist education would benefit her drifting son, Mrs. Crane lost no time in trying once again to arrange it for him, and a few days after he returned from Easton in late December or early January, she shipped him off to Syracuse University. Under its chancellor, the Reverend Charles N. Sims, Syracuse had maintained the moral rigor insisted on by its Methodist founders, one of whom was Mrs. Crane's uncle, Bishop Jesse T. Peck. Like Pennington Seminary, it was an ideal institution for Mrs. Crane's purposes. What Stephen thought about it at the time is not known, but he was probably not altogether displeased. His brother Townley had arranged a job for him as the *Tribune*'s Syracuse correspondent. This assignment, and the fact that the University had a lively baseball team, made the idea of another sally into higher education at least tolerable. He was also allowed to enroll as a special student in the Scientific Course, which gave him the privilege of choosing subjects as he pleased. But the main attraction was baseball. "They used to say at Syracuse University, where, by the way, I didn't finish the course, that I was cut out to be a professional base-ball player. And the truth of the matter is that I went there more to play base-ball than to study."[37]

He registered January 6, transferred his Delta Upsilon membership from Lafayette and, according to his mother's plan, moved into Bishop Peck's widow's house. But the Widow Peck was not happy with her great-nephew's ideas about life and living, and after a few days he moved, first to a boarding house and then shortly to the Delta Upsilon fraternity house, where he arrived one day, as a friend reported, "in a cab and cloud of tobacco smoke." "The ΔY Chapter here," he wrote his Claverack friends, "has got a dandy house valued at $20,000.00, situated on a high hill over-looking the entire city. As I said before to Sioux there are certainly some dam pretty girls here, praised be to God. . . . [This is a] dandy city at least and I expect to see some fun here."[38]

Impressions of him vary, of course, but friends who described him about this time generally agree on certain personal traits. He was about medium height, slightly built, sallow in complexion, and careless in dress and grooming. Slow and deliberate in his movements, he spoke in a soft lazy drawl; and though often moodily uncommunicative, he could on occasion talk with extraordinary fluency and originality. More than one of his classmates noted his kindness and consideration, finding in him, as Frank Noxon did, "a haunting solicitude for the comfort and welfare of other people, especially those of narrow means."[39] Like his father, he was extremely fond of animals, especially horses and dogs. He once told someone that he automatically trusted anyone who showed affection for dogs.

At Syracuse he was predictably indifferent to academic opportunities. He attended lectures so seldom, in fact, that a story developed that only one student ever remembered seeing him in a classroom, a youngster who admired him for his baseball abilities and who found his presence memorable for this reason.[40] Professor Frank Smalley, to whom Mrs. Crane wrote several times inquiring anxiously about him, called him in for a talk. "We looked upon him as an exceedingly bright young man, of large capacity," he wrote. "[But] he would not be cramped following a course of study he did not care for."[41] He and Norton Goodwin, with whom he shared a room in the Delta Upsilon house, and their friends Frederic Lawrence and Clarence Peaslee defied "the grim Methodist environment" by attending the theater, drinking, keeping late hours, and playing hearts, fan-tan, and poker. When Miss Frances Willard, the noted reformer, came to visit, he

declined to meet her on the grounds that she was a fool. "Frances Willard," he wrote once, "is one of those wonderful people who can tell right from wrong for everybody from the polar cap to the equator. Perhaps it never struck her that people differ from her. I have loved myself passionately now and then but Miss Willard's affair with Miss Willard should be stopped by the police."[42] His friend Lawrence reported that he had "fierce contempt" for the faculty, except for Charles J. Little, Professor of History and Logic, though it was Professor Little who called him to his desk one day after an examination on the French Revolution and told him that he "was going very wrong indeed."[43] When one of his professors chided him for an unorthodox idea by reminding him of St. Paul's position on the question, Crane replied, as the story has it, "I know what St. Paul said, but I disagree with St. Paul." About this time he was also saying, "There is nothing save opinion—and opinion be damned."[44]

His reputation as a baseball player had preceded him, and even before the practice for the new season began, the school newspaper noted that "Crane, the old catcher of the Lafayette College team, has entered the University and will make a good addition to the team." He played "with a fiendish glee"; quick and excitable on the diamond, he was in ceaseless motion, talkative, "wantonly profane," acidly sarcastic when teammates made poor plays but generous with praise when they made good ones.[45] He did not like the heavy mitt which was just then coming into use, preferring instead a padded glove; the pitcher, Mansfield French, was a large man who threw extraordinarily fast balls, and when the lightly built Crane caught for him, every ball seemed to lift him off his feet and propel him bodily backwards.

One of his friends thought he seemed indifferent to everything but baseball, but in this the friend was mistaken. He haunted the police station and the slums and appeared regularly in the back room of a local restaurant to talk about his experiences. The police court, he said, was the most interesting place in the city. In the cupola of the Delta Upsilon house, furnished with a rug and other exotic appointments, he read, smoked his Turkish water pipe, and lounged with friends in "true oriental fashion, talking for long hours of science, art, literature. . . ."[46] He was fond of paintings and had several in his room, according to one visitor, who also noted that it was the untidiest room in the house.

He was also writing regularly. He worked hard on a story about a dog named Jack, which the editor of *St. Nicholas* rejected, though with kind words of praise; and he wrote a somewhat anti-Semitic dramatic sketch, "Greed Rampant," a story in which scheming Gentiles lure Jews out of choice places in heaven ("Paradise, New Jersey") by circulating false reports of bargain real estate on the outside. His first published fiction, "The King's Favor," appeared in the Syracuse literary magazine, the *University Herald*, in May, a comical story about an African chief who tries to give a touring New York tenor one of his wives as a token of royal appreciation for his singing. He also began a story about a prostitute, pages of which he left scattered about on the floor of his room, where visitors picked them up and read them. Some of his friends later thought this story was an early version of *Maggie: A Girl of the Streets*, based on observations of life in the Syracuse tenement district, though *Maggie* as it was published in 1893 was almost certainly begun at the earliest in the late fall of 1891, after Crane had begun exploring the Bowery and tenements of lower Manhattan.

His keen eye for the incongruous and his quick sense of the absurd are shown in "Great Bugs of Onondaga," an article which appeared in the *New York Tribune* and *Syracuse Sunday Herald* in June. Inspired by a story in the *Herald* about caterpillars swarming on railroad tracks and stalling trains in Minnesota, Crane concocted a whimsical deadpan story about how a "wild-eyed man in overalls" had come in from the country to report that "strange insects of immense proportion" had covered railroad tracks near an outlying mine and rendered a locomotive helpless. These great bugs, "about the size and shape of half a shanghai-egg shell," were, according to a local "erudite recluse," a "rare species of lithodome—a rock-boring mollusk—crossed with some kind of predatory insect." Some, Crane wrote, huddled on the track and lay perfectly still while others played "a sort of leapfrog over their fellows' backs."[47] This spirited joke created a stir of editorial amusement. Willis Johnson, in an editorial in the *Tribune*, solemnly offered an elaborate evolutionary hypothesis, and the editor of the *Syracuse Daily Standard* also printed the story with an accompanying editorial comment.

When the term ended in June, Crane went back to Asbury Park to help Townley with vacation news gathering, as he had been doing every summer since 1888. As for college, a statement he made a few years later expressed fairly well his feeling about it in 1891. "I did little work at school, but confined my abilities, such as they were, to the diamond. Not that I disliked books, but the cut-and-dried curriculum of the college did not appeal to me. Humanity was a much more interesting study. When I ought to have been at recitations I was studying faces on the streets, and when I ought to have been studying my next day's lessons I was watching the trains roll in and out of the Central Station. So, you see, I had, first of all, to recover from college. I had to build up, so to speak."[48] He had decided to be a writer, and he knew when he left Syracuse in June that he would not return. College, he was sure, had very little to do with the kind of writer he wanted to be.

T W O

A S B U R Y   P A R K

WHEN CRANE returned to Asbury Park in early June of 1891 to take up his duties as a seasonal reporter, Townley apparently all but turned the *Tribune* column over to him. From the agency's headquarters at the Lake Avenue Hotel, he wandered the beach, sometimes with his Syracuse friend Arthur Oliver, another cub reporter, or with Ralph Paine of the Asbury Park *Journal*, in search of bits and pieces of shore news and items for human interest paragraphs.

His friend Paine thought it remarkable that this "youth with the soul of a poet and a psychologist" should find "even in that futile, inconsequential environment of Asbury Park in midsummer" encouragement for his literary ambitions.[1] On the contrary, it would be hard to imagine a better situation for the education of a young writer with Crane's gift for observation and inborn sense of irony. It was a lively scene, "the best news centre on the entire New Jersey coast," Townley once wrote. The free-spending life of the family vacationers in the resort hotels, the devoted worship of the religious conferees at Ocean Grove, and the earnest pursuit of culture and self-improvement at Avon-by-the-Sea provided sharp contrasts and contradictions. As Crane was shortly to realize now that he had begun to look upon this world as a potential literary scene, these communities comprised a neat microcosm of American life, concentrating tendencies, often violently antithetical, in the nation's religious, cultural, and social life.

Largely owned and governed by the eccentric, genteel millionaire James A. Bradley, Asbury Park was created for wholesome amusement. It attracted affluent businessmen who brought their wives and daughters to enjoy the comforts of the resort hotels, the innocent pleasures of the amusement park, the music hall, and the beach. But it drew many other types, as Crane noted: the "sharp, keen-looking New-York business man, the long and lank Jersey farmer, the dark-skinned sons of India, the self-possessed Chinaman, the black-haired Southerner and the man with the big hat from 'the wild and woolly plains' of the West."[2] At the height of the season as many as 15,000 people could be seen strolling in the evenings on the big boardwalk that extended along the ocean front to Ocean Grove a mile or so south.

Life at Ocean Grove was regulated, at least in theory, by strict Methodist discipline. The approved activities were churchgoing and religious meditation. "Donkey and soap-bubble parties," Crane wrote, "are the only amusements enjoyed here openly."[3] Novels, indecorous bathing suits, and dancing were forbidden. The great auditorium, where from July 4 to the end of the season in August "the soul hungry for intellectual pablum" (as Crane had once put it) could "feast to its fulness,"[4] accommodated congregations of seven or eight thousand. During the summer season ministers assembled for great conferences and revivals, and prominent workers in reform and missionary enterprises, like Mrs. Crane, attended as speakers, organizers, and teachers.

Also on Crane's beat was Avon-by-the-Sea, a center for culture and learning on the beach just below Ocean Grove. The Seaside Assembly, as its elaborate summer school was called, brought in prominent artists, lecturers, and teachers to hold Chautauqua-like seminars in science, literature, and the arts. The Assembly was very popular with vacationers who wished to combine pleasure and self-improvement; and in 1891 its program was greatly expanded to include classes in biology, mathematics, political science, languages, American literature, Bible study, art, writing, and music.

But as everyone knew, there was a hidden life in this community of innocence on the Jersey coast. There were clandestine poker games in the great resort hotels and liquor in back rooms of drugstores and tobacco shops, as Mrs. Crane had noted sadly in the mid-eighties in an article in a local newspaper, though an even more serious threat, she had complained, was the temptation of idle amusements. "In this beautiful place," she wrote, "it is not the avowed skeptic, the open grog-shop, or the gambling hell that Christians are called upon to combat, but it is the growing taste for worldly amusements which keeps the young from the house of God, dissipating religious convictions. . . ."[5] But in recent years the grog-shop and gambling hell had become more troublesome and the proprietor of Asbury Park, the redoubtable James A. Bradley, known as "Founder" Bradley, had ordered the police to conduct annual raids on offending drugstores and hotels.

What Crane observed as he made his way up and down the beach was the effect on ordinary daily life of the clash between the lingering faith and innocent piety of an older America and the brash secularism of the new. In the trivial events of resort life he could see often the precarious balance struck between idle pleasure and moral discipline, self-improvement and self-indulgence, faith and skepticism, Christian humility and worldly vanity; and in these uneasy, contradictory, and uncertain balances he discovered much to stimulate his natural gift for irony. "As an intellectual personality," Arthur Oliver wrote, " 'Stevie' Crane always impressed me as very old for his years when we were young chaps together down on the Jersey shore. Beneath a somewhat diffident exterior, he had a keen sense of the real meaning of things. He saw and felt deeply. Even as a boy, he had a richly developed vein of satire."[6]

He had first become fully aware of the literary possibilities of the scene the year before, as the articles he wrote for the *Tribune* in the summer of 1890 show. They single out the comically officious "Founder" Bradley, one of the more bizarre personalities of the community, as a model of personal conceit and moral complacency. They identify the shallow, self-centered "summer girl" and her yearning suitor, "the golden youth," as types of mindless vanity. They bristle with odd and revealing juxtapositions, like the exquisitely gowned "summer girl" posing against the background of the sombre ocean, chewing gum energetically in time with the rolling surf (a first, faint intimation of his sense of man's poignant alienation in nature, one of the major themes of his work). They picture poker players in Asbury Park rattling their chips as they listen to far-off sounds from Ocean Grove of "5,000 throats singing the doxology."[7]

There are hints in these earliest writings of attitudes which were to become fixed and characteristic. He was suspicious of philosophical abstractions, pretentious examples of which he had found in the inflated language and complacent air of members of the American Institute of Christian Philosophy. Ordinary hotel guests, Crane wrote, "claim that they can tell the members of the institute from afar by a certain wise, grave and reverend air that hangs over them from the top of their glossy silk hats to their equally glossy boots. A member gazes at the wild tossing of the waves with a calm air of understanding and philosophy that the poor youthful graduate from college . . . can never hope to acquire. When [the philosopher] learns to row on the lake or river, to his philosophical mind he is only describing an arc from the rowlock as a centre, with a radius equal to the distance between the fulcrum or rowlock and the point of resistance, vulgarly known as the tip end of the oar." This same philosopher, who scorns the trivial hotel "hops" and watches from the sidelines with patronizing amusement "has no doubt in his own mind, from certain little geometric calculations of his own, that he could waltz in such a scientific manner, with such an application of the laws of motion, that the best dancers would, indeed, be surprised."[8]

Another paragraph describes the awe in which the elderly retired businessman, "wending his way with his books to the Hall of Philosophy to take a lesson in French, or to Otis Hall to study art," holds education. One enthusiastic old pupil "put[s] his hand on a young man's head and say[s]: 'My boy, study hard; don't give up your books. How much more I might have been in the world if I had thought more of my Caesar's Commentaries and my geometry than I did of sleighride parties and corn huskings.'" "In Madame Alberti's classes in physical culture," Crane had observed, "it is interesting to note the look of surprise on people's faces, many of them showing the marks of age, when they learn for the first time the proper way to pick up articles from the floor or the scientific method of taking a chair, or, as an old farmer said to a friend, when asked how he liked the lecture, 'I'm going on sixty-six-year-old, an' I never knew how to shet a door or git out'n a wagon before.'"[9]

Now, in 1891, having decided to be a writer, he resumed these literary exercises with a sense of new purpose. The dozen-and-a-half articles he wrote that summer show a bolder style, more confident and more consciously literary. Observing the turmoil among the hotel porters occasioned by the sudden arrival of heavily laden cabs and carriages, he practiced describing the comical confusion and disorder of excitable crowds, a constantly recurring image in his later work. He experimented with the ironic effects of contrasts between the "turmoil" of the mob and the serenity "of a long, quiet avenue shaded by waving maples, with a vision of blue sea in the distance."[10] He tested odd epithets and visual effects, noting that pleasure parties on nearby Shark River "create havoc among the blithesome crabs and the festive oysters" and that the white umbrellas of a party of picnickers give "the appearance of a bunch of extraordinary mushrooms."[11]

In these tentative experiments with themes, attitudes, and expression, Crane showed an uncanny ability to anticipate his literary future. In an account of the wreck of the sailing ship *New Era* off the shore at Asbury Park in 1869, he described graphically the suffering and despair of survivors clinging to the rigging of the foundering ship and falling one by one into the raging sea in full view of a crowd watching helplessly from the beach—a remarkable anticipation of incident and perspective in "The Open Boat."[12] He also tried his hand at a story about the Far West, intending, as it appears from two unfinished manuscript fragments, a parody of the type made popular by Bret Harte and the dime novel. It was to be about the deadly rivalry between two wild Arizona towns, Apache Crossing and Blazer; the characters, apparently, were to be stock figures: suave and soft-spoken gamblers, "leathery cowboys," and "noted fighters and desperados of Arizona."[13] These fragments are the first in a long series of Western tales leading to the superb late stories "The Bride Comes to Yellow Sky" and "The Blue Hotel."

In August occurred the first important event of his literary career. "Professor" Hamlin Garland, an enthusiastic, radical-minded young writer and critic from Boston, delivered a series of lectures on American literature at the Seaside Assembly at Avon in July and August, and one afternoon in late August Crane appeared to cover his lecture on William Dean Howells. Garland read Crane's report in the *Tribune* the next day and asked William M. Alberti, the dean of the Assembly, for the name of the author. "He is a mere boy," Alberti told him, "and his name is Stephen Crane." Garland sent for him and Crane shortly appeared, "a reticent young fellow, with a big German pipe in his mouth. He was small, sallow and inclined to stoop, but sinewy and athletic for all that."[14] They talked baseball and Crane came several times before Garland left Avon to catch his pitches and theorize about "inshoots" and "outshoots." Neither ever mentioned that they used these occasions to talk about writing, but in view both of Garland's intense preoccupation with theories of art and literature and his dedication to the new realism (or "veritism" as he called his own aesthetic program) and of Crane's recent resolve to be a writer, it seems likely that they did. Garland was just becoming known as a writer. His *Main-Travelled Roads*, a collection of realistic stories about life on the great Western prairies, had appeared less than two months before, and he was well established as a contributor to the prestigious *Harper's Weekly* and B. O. Flower's radical Boston magazine, the *Arena*. To Crane, this intense, self-assured young man was an admirable example of the radical new writer, and though Garland's own pedestrian fiction could have been of little interest to Crane, he would have surely found the lecturer's avant-garde theories of art and literature impressive. Garland was almost certainly one of the earliest and most important influences on Crane's development as a writer.

From his reading of Hippolyte Taine, Herbert Spencer, and Henry George, the self-educated Garland had become an ardent advocate of the theory of evolution and had worked some of its premises into sweeping theories about art, literature, and society. From the idea that evolution ensures a constant unfolding of new and better forms in society and the arts as well as in nature, he devised theories of painting, fiction, and drama that emphasized the importance of the new—new styles, new subjects, new forms. The only true subject, he declared, was contemporary American life: true art reflects progress toward heterogeneity, and thus the art of the future must reflect, in obedience to this law, the immense variety of color and movement in the broad national scene, in the big city, the slums, the remote prairies.

From Eugène Véron's *Aesthetics*, Garland adopted ideas, which he apparently passed on to Crane, about the fundamental relation of personality to representation in art. Véron insisted that the proper function of the artist is to represent the observed fact as he responds to it affectively, not as he might suppose it to exist objectively. Mere realism—the objective representation of fact—is sterile; only the observer's unique impression of a fact gives it its significance—or even its reality. Véron's idea that new forms are inevitably created by the true artist's individual vision meshed well with Garland's evolutionary theory of art, justifying his rejection of the attitudes and conventions in the art of the past. "There are but three ways open to art," Véron wrote in a passage which summarizes his aesthetic theory: "the imitation of previous forms of art; the realistic imitation of actual things; the manifestation of individual impressions." Only the last, he said, is valid, for "the determinant and essential constituent of art is the personality of the artist."[15]

Garland absorbed these ideas and freely adapted them to his theory of art and expression. In an 1890 essay on Ibsen in the *Arena* he had declared that realism "has only one law, to be true, not to the objective reality, but to the objective reality *as the author sees it*."[16] And Crane about this time was advising his friend Arthur Oliver on the subject. "Somehow," Oliver complained about a story he was writing, "I can't get down to the real thing. . . . I get all tangled up with different notions of how it ought to be told." Crane picked up a handful of sand and tossed it in the breeze. "Treat your notions like that," he said. "Forget what you think about it and tell how you feel about it. . . . That's the big secret of story-telling. Away with literary fads and canons. Be yourself."[17]

Crane as a rule showed little respect for theories, but as this colloquialization of Véron's aesthetics suggests, he could adapt theory to his program easily enough if it happened to come his way in a time of need. For his concept of art, he was undoubtedly indebted to Garland, and, in quite a different way, to Kipling. Kipling's immensely popular *The Light That Failed* began appearing in *Lippincott's* magazine in January, 1891, and Crane probably read it in the cupola of the Delta Upsilon house at Syracuse, where he spent many afternoons that winter and spring reading and writing and "developing his style," as he said. But whenever he read it, Kipling's novel made a powerful impression on him, as later adaptation of its images of baleful red suns in the famous red-sun-as-water image in *The Red Badge of Courage* suggests. The hero of Kipling's novel, Dick Heldar, must have represented all that this twenty-year-old youth hoped to become. Dick is a realist painter and newspaper artist in sharp revolt against genteel art and sterile canons of respectability. He is a free-living Bohemian who finds "unvarnished" truths in the violence of slums and battlefields. He chooses to suffer poverty and hardship in the slums because he thinks "the belly-pinch of hunger" will make him a better artist. The novel bristles with talk about art and color. "What color that was!" Dick exclaims, describing his adventures in the exotic Sudan. "Opal and umber and amber and claret and brick-red and sulphur—cocatoo-crest sulphur—against brown, with a nigger-black rock sticking up in the middle of it all, and a decorative frieze of camels festooning in front of a pure pale turquoise sky."[18] Crane would shortly be trying out such color effects in some of his stories about outdoor life in the Sullivan County sketches. He would also shortly, like Dick Heldar, turn to war and poverty for subjects and test the sentimental theory of deprivation as a stimulus to artistic creativity. Thus by the end of the season of 1891 he had a theory and a program for action.

In mid-June he went off to Port Jervis, where he joined his Syracuse friend Frederic Lawrence and two other outdoorsmen, Louis Senger and Louis Carr, on a camping trip to Sullivan County. They roamed the rugged terrain by day and sat around huge campfires talking and smoking half the night. Crane, companionable and entertaining, as Lawrence recalled, was "very happy," as he always seemed to be on these expeditions. In August, probably shortly after meeting Garland, he joined the group again for four weeks in the woods of Pike County, Pennsylvania. They slept on the ground "like true savages," Lawrence said, and the sun burned Crane's skin a deep copper, "almost like that of an American Indian."[19]

At Asbury Park he met Helen Trent, a tall, dark young woman passing the summer at one of the resort hotels before setting off to London in the fall to marry a young English physician. By the time she returned to New York to pack leisurely for the voyage, Crane was in love with her. Not knowing about the London physician, he followed her. He rode the ferry across the Hudson from his brother Ed's house in Lake View to call on her at the elaborate old Manhattan mansion which, he was shocked to learn, had once been occupied by the mistress of an Irish politician, a fact he anxiously revealed to her. He told her about his recent adventures in the Bowery and the East Side tenement districts and of his ambitions to write a book about them one day. He talked about Hamlin Garland, who, he said, was "like a nice Jesus Christ," and expressed other angular views and opinions. Christianity, he said, was "mildewed." And the Bowery he found the most interesting place in New York, echoing perhaps the journalist Julian Ralph, whose graphic description of the infamous street he may have seen in the *Century* a few weeks earlier. Helen and her young lover quarrelled, probably about the Bowery, which she thought "not nice," and Crane left angrily. Then, remorseful, he wrote a note from the ferry: "I shall come back tomorrow night and we can start all over again." Once, refused admission, he stood miserably in the street, watching her house. "Your window was lighted all last night," he wrote her, "but they said you were not in. I stood and looked at your window until a policeman came and made me go away. But I came back and looked until my head was just a sponge of lights."[20] One evening she found the courage to tell him about the London physician, and Crane wheeled abruptly and left the house without a word.

Mrs. Crane died in December, and he now made Ed's house in Lake View his nominal home, though he spent much time in the city that fall and winter, staying over in hotels and rooming houses to study the streets and tenements around the derelict-strewn Bowery. Garland had no doubt encouraged him to continue these studies, begun earlier in the Syracuse tenements, for Crane would have heard his August lecture at Avon on the coming role of the city in American fiction and would almost certainly have read his description of Boston slum life in his "Under the Wheel," a play published in the *Arena* in 1890 and recast later as the novel *Jason Edwards.*

His life in the city was almost as hard as that of the people he studied. With no certain income, living hand to mouth, he was often obliged to retreat to Ed's house, sometimes in near-desperate circumstances, as a scribbled note suggests: "Please send me $5 by this bearer whose name is only Smith. Am going to Ed's at Lakeview and need some grub. Otherwise I shall eat the front door, his baby and the cat."[21] At Ed's he played baseball and football with the neighborhood teams; football, he would claim later, gave him the sense of rage and conflict which he drew on for battle scenes in *The Red Badge of Courage.* But he was writing then about something else—Sullivan County—and in the winter and spring of 1892 he wrote half a dozen articles for the *Tribune* on its history and legends. Except for an occasional flash of wit or striking image, as in his description of the rugged country as a landscape formed by a "very reckless and distracted giant" who tossed boulders around and smashed out gullies willy-nilly,[22] these pieces are not distinguished in style. Nevertheless, Crane was contemplating fame in literature and even anticipating its perils. In early 1892, or perhaps late 1891, he wrote an unfinished draft of "In the Country of Rhymers and Writers," an allegorical fantasy about the troubles writers have with hostile critics and a dull and indifferent public.[23] Crane's concern seems curiously premature, but it accurately predicted an aspect of his future and confirmed in some way, no doubt, his commitment to it.

In May he was in Sullivan County again with his camping friends, but when it rained four days straight, they returned to Port Jervis, and Crane left a legend carved on a tree: "Allah il Allah! And it rained forty days and forty nights." At Ed's house he worked on a series of little stories based on these camping experiences and then went to Syracuse for a short visit before reporting to Townley in Asbury Park in mid-June to begin another summer of paragraph writing for the *Tribune*.

This season he had even more freedom in the *Tribune* column than before. Townley, more interested in poker at the hotels than in the details of his brilliant young brother's literary experiments, apparently left the whole business in Stephen's hands. As what he wrote shows, he was more aware than ever before of the literary possibilities of the scene; and now in possession of a bolder, more fluent and supple style, he gave his satirical impulses full reign. With irreverent irony and enthusiastic hyperbole he pictured crowds of preachers, socialites, entertainers, and stolid businessmen flowing across the boulevards and boardwalks seeking pleasures, publicity, or spiritual enrichment. "In the evening," he wrote of the resort scene in a passage which anticipates street scenes in *Maggie*, "it is a glare of light and a swirl of gayly attired women and well-dressed men." This world of people "is situated somewhere under the long line of electric lights which dangles over the great cosmopolitan thoroughfare. It is the world of the middle classes; add but princes and gamblers and it would be what the world calls the world."[24]

The contrast between glamour in Asbury Park and piety in Ocean Grove is skillfully drawn. Describing preachers gathering at Ocean Grove for a religious conference, he wrote that "sombre-hued gentlemen . . . are arriving in solemn procession, with black valises in their hands and rebukes to frivolity in their eyes. They greet each other with quiet enthusiasm and immediately set about holding meetings."[25] At the resort, by contrast, "pleasure-seekers arrive by the avalanche" and descend on the amusement park where they find a new "razzle-dazzle" (which is, "of course, a moral machine") and an upright wheel. "This will revolve, carrying little cars, to be filled evidently with desperate persons, around and around, up and down."[26] In a later report he describes the inevitable confrontation between vacationer and religionist: the somber-hued gentlemen came and complained "that the steam organ disturbed their pious meditations on the evils of the world. Thereupon the minions of the law violently suppressed the wheel and its attendants."[27]

Certain character types observed on the great boardwalk he saw as studies in vanity. The "average summer guest" he identified as a middle-class innocent whose comical egotism makes him a helpless victim of wily hotel proprietors. "The average summer guest," he wrote, "stands in his two shoes with American self-reliance and, playing casually with his watch-chain, looks at the world with a clear eye." He is certain of his vast worldly knowledge even as he foolishly submits to the "arrogant prices" of the resort hotels; "he will pay fancy prices for things with a great unconcern. However, deliberately and baldly attempt to beat him out of fifteen cents and he will put his hands in his pockets, spread his legs apart and wrangle, in a loud voice, until sundown. . . ."[28] Two exemplars of comical vanity who had appeared in sketches the year before are discovered in more elaborate roles: the vain "golden youth," a "rose-tint and gilt-edge" swaggerer who appears on the beach with his narcissistic "summer girl, a bit of interesting tinsel flashing near the sombre-hued waves."[29] And the pompous and officious "founder" Bradley, who "wears a white sun-umbrella with a green lining and has very fierce and passionate whiskers. . . ."[30] He posts signs all around the ocean front, a large stretch of which he owns, to advertise his standards of piety and gentility and to caution guests against unseemly conduct on his beaches. "It warms his heart to see the thousands of people tramping over his boards, helter-skeltering in his sand and diving into that ocean of the Lord's which is adjacent to the beach of James A. Bradley."[31]

Willis Johnson, day editor of the *Tribune* and old friend of the Crane family, was vacationing in Asbury Park that summer. Learning from Townley that Stephen had written several stories based on his camping and hunting adventures in Sullivan County, Johnson asked to see them, and Crane brought him two, probably "Four Men in a Cave" and "The Octopush." The editor bought them for the Sunday feature page of the *Tribune*, where they, and three more he bought later, appeared in July.[32] There were ten in all, though only five appeared in the *Tribune*.

The hero of these "little grotesque tales of the woods," as Crane once described them, is the nearly anonymous "little man" who wanders through the fields and forests of Sullivan County with his three camping friends challenging what he perceives as an inimical spirit of nature, sinister powers of an alien and hostile world. He confronts a cave "because its black mouth had gaped at him."[33] He is enraged when a "mesmeric" mountain seems to glower at him, and he "conquers" it by scrambling furiously to its summit.[34] He cowers in abject terror at the wailing of a demon in the haunted night[35] and is petrified with fear when a "ghoul" snatches him away from his glowering campfire.[36] But this malevolence in nature, as Crane's irony constantly reveals, is an illusion, a creation of the little man's morbid anxieties. The cave's black mouth is actually nothing more than "a little tilted hole" on a hillside; the awful cry of the phantom is only the howling of a starving dog; the baleful mountain, once "mastered," simply a stolid, indifferent hill, "motionless under his feet"; and the ghoul is only an ignorant potato farmer who wants him to add a column of figures for him.

The tales show little concern for objective realism. The drama is in the little man's mind, which transmutes the reality of nature into dreamlike imagery of anxiety and vain delusion. The world he sees as threatening, tenderly benign, or maddeningly enigmatic is merely a projection of mental lights and shades. The sun sinking behind the treetops is the face of an angry man peering over a hedge; the clammy floor of a dark tunnel leading into a cave seems "alive and writhing" and "traitorous rocks" bruise his hands and knees; a campfire glowers and hates the world, and dusky night comes near to "menace" him and fight battles with the flare of the dying fire. The sentient pines huddle together and sing in the whirling wind, and on a ridge-top "a dismal choir of hemlocks" croon over one that has fallen. During a long, serene afternoon of pickerel fishing, when the sun gleams "merrily" on the water, the landscape is a pastoral idyll, though the little man, peering into the sinister depths of the lake, notes "millions of fern branches" that "quavered and hid mysteries."[37]

Inconsequential though they may be in themselves, these odd, anecdotal pieces reveal much about the development of Crane's style and imagination. Their preoccupation with an animistic nature, obliquely derived from his puritan sense of a fallen world, probably owed much to Bishop Peck's descriptions of a devil-haunted world in his lurid treatise on sin and salvation, *What Must I Do to Be Saved?* Crane's feeling for the consequences of delusion and vanity was also derived ultimately from Christian doctrine, but more immediately from his Asbury Park studies of the comically narcissistic "summer girl," the deluded "average summer guest," and the lordly, presumptuous James A. Bradley. In their arresting metaphors, quick, shallow treatment of action and incident, and gaudy dramatic coloring, they show all the excesses of the Sunday supplement prose of the time; but they show too that he was rapidly discovering the situations, actions, incidents, and language of the unique patterns of his later composition. From the Sullivan County sketches on, he husbanded particular metaphors, phrases, images, and motifs and used them again and again in a wide range of variation. Sunset, glaring lights, shadows, pompous oratorical postures and utterances, banal sentiments mockingly expressed in banal language, atmospheres charged with feelings of threat and imminent crisis are all features of his writing from beginning to end. In the Sullivan County sketches, to trace only one example, the battles between the animistic dusk of night and the red glare of campfires and setting suns become the campfires glowing against the threatening dark in *The Red Badge of Courage*. In *George's Mother* the same imagery describes the play of crimson light from shop windows on the vaguely sinister shadows of city streets. In the Greek war dispatches the trope becomes the flickering, uncertain campfires around which Greek soldiers croon (like the doleful pines in the Sullivan County sketches) their weird native songs. And in the Cuban dispatches the campfires of peasant insurgents flare fitfully in the deep jungle night where lurks the terrible Spanish guerrilla. Many of the details of image and metaphor in these first stories become in time the unmistakable signatures of his style.

He played baseball through the summer and strolled abroad with Lily Brandon Munroe, a young married woman living in one of the hotels with her mother-in-law and young sister Dottie. Her husband, a geologist, was away on an extended business trip. Crane took her to Daly's for ice cream (which he did not like), to the amusement park to ride the merry-go-round, and for long walks along the beach. Though not happily married and genuinely attracted to Crane, she was nevertheless cautious and prudent in her relationship with him. She was touched by the intensity of his feelings, but she also thought he was too impractical and visionary. And she worried about his bad eating habits, incessant smoking, and hacking cough. She probably thought he was right when he told her that he did not expect to live long. Within a few months, long before he recovered from his infatuation, Crane wrote (with remarkable detachment, under the circumstances) a deft little comedy, "The Pace of Youth," which tells of the romance between Frank, a merry-go-round attendant, and Lizzie, the comely ticket girl.[38] Their touching courtship, set against the great ocean and the grand sweep of the night sky, is described with wry and tender irony. The story clearly draws heavily on his affair with Lily.

One day in late August, Crane filed a story with the *Tribune* which abruptly ended the Asbury Park phase of his career. Townley, away at a funeral, as he claimed later, assigned Stephen to cover the parade of the Junior Order of United American Mechanics, an organization of patriotic working men who assembled annually at Asbury Park to parade through the town and spend a day at the amusement park and on the beach. Crane, leaning in the doorway of a billiard parlor, observed with deep interest the contrast between these "bronzed, slope-shouldered, uncouth and begrimed" men of the working class and the throng of Asbury Park spectators "composed of summer gowns, lace parasols, tennis trousers, straw hats and indifferent smiles." He went immediately to Townley's office in the Lake Avenue Hotel and wrote a vivid, sardonic description of the event. The Juniors, he noted, had no proper idea of marching. "It was probably the most awkward, ungainly, uncut and uncarved procession that ever raised clouds of dust on sun-beaten streets." But this rabble of hundreds of marchers, plodding along to the "furious discords" of brass bands, were men of "tan-colored, sun-beaten honesty," unlike the "bona fide Asbury Parker . . . to whom a dollar, when held close to his eye, often shuts out any impression he may have had that other people possess rights"; and this crowd of summer idlers found vaguely amusing these "spraddle-legged men . . . whose hands were bent and shoulders stooped from delving and constructing. . . ."[39]

The article caused a minor crisis in the editorial offices at the *Tribune*. Politicians had been busy all that summer wooing the labor vote, and one of them was Whitelaw Reid, owner and editor-in-chief of the *Tribune* and candidate for Vice President of the United States on the Republican ticket with Benjamin Harrison. When rival Democratic editors saw Crane's piece, they gleefully cited its unflattering picture of the marchers as evidence of the *Tribune*'s secret bias against labor. Reid received a warm letter of protest from an officer of the JOUAM complaining that Crane's article had insulted their organization. Reid ordered his editor, Willis Johnson, to print a retraction and an apology and to fire Townley and Stephen Crane. Garland, who was lecturing at the Assembly again that year, recalled that Crane, much distressed, appeared shortly after the article came out and told him that the *Tribune* had "given him the bounce." When Oliver called to cheer him up, Crane greeted him "with a saintly smile he always had ready for every disaster." Crane wrote nothing else for the *Tribune*, and Townley, who was becoming somewhat notorious as an eccentric and alcoholic, ended his career, William said, a broken man.

Stephen retired to William's house in Port Jervis, where this stolid older brother was now well established as a lawyer and leading citizen, known locally as "Judge" Crane. Then in the last days of the summer he was off to Pike County with Frederic Lawrence and other outdoorsmen on the big annual camping expedition. When he returned in the fall, he was ready for something new. He was not happy with the Sullivan County sketches, which he thought too much influenced by Rudyard Kipling's superficial irony and flippant humor, and he was now determined to give up this "clever school in literature." It seemed to him now that "there must be something more in life than to sit and cudgel one's brains for clever and witty expedients."[40] Garland's ideas, and Howells's as Garland had presented them in his Seaside Assembly lectures, had enlarged his conception of the significance of the art of fiction. The proper aim of a writer, as he now understood it, was to bring the issues of common social life into sharp, critical focus through the powers of aesthetic forms. "So I developed all alone a little creed of art which I thought was a good one," he wrote Lily. "Later I discovered that my creed was identical with the one of Howells and Garland and in this way I became involved in the beautiful war between those who say art is man's substitute for nature [and truth] . . . and those who say—well, I don't know what they say. They don't, they can't say much but they fight villianously and keep Garland and I out of the big magazines."[41]

Obviously, fact suffers as much in this as grammar and spelling. He had known about Howells's and Garland's theories at least since 1891; and though he was glad to espouse their views that literature is the truthful representation of experience, his "program," if he was indeed conscious of one beyond these expansive generalizations, was not like theirs, as a comparison of a page from *Maggie* with one from, say, Howells's "An East Side

Ramble" (1890) or Garland's *Jason Edwards* (1892) would demonstrate. Crane could have had vaguely in mind a "little creed of art" he had "devised" out of the long stretches of talk about art and nature in Kipling's *The Light That Failed*, but he was mainly posturing for Lily. Years later he sent Howells an inscribed copy of *The Red Badge of Courage* "as a token of the veneration and gratitude of Stephen Crane for many things he has learned of the common man and, above all, for a certain re-adjustment of his point of view victoriously concluded some time in 1892."[42] Crane's "program," though, was his own—and less a program, as *Maggie* would show, than an intuitive expression of his own unique perceptions and attitudes. He was probably not fully aware that in these he was very different from Howells. When he returned from camp at the end of the summer of 1892, he was apparently contemplating a future as a social realist, and in October he plunged into the Bohemian life of East Side Manhattan, resolved to capture for literature the color and movement of life in the big city.

THREE

NEW YORK

IN OCTOBER Crane was in Manhattan, living on Avenue A with a crowd of medical students in a shabby old house presided over by a landlady whose mildly tyrannical edicts and adjurations earned her the sobriquet "the dragon." He shared a rear room with Frederic Lawrence, his friend from Syracuse days, now in his last year of medical studies. From their window they could look out over a jumble of tenement roofs to the East River and Blackwell's Island, where they could just make out lines of lockstepping convicts in the yard of the massive prison—a detail Crane would shortly work into the composition of *Maggie*. He christened the boarding house "The Pendennis Club," presumably a reference to Thackeray's novel, though the meaning is unclear.

While Lawrence worked at his medical studies, Crane roamed the tenement districts and lounged about the room, smoking, writing, and reading. Lawrence remembered that their bare library included *Candide*, a volume of Maupassant, and Zola's *Pot-bouille*. Zola's novel, and perhaps his earlier *L'Assommoir*, may have sharpened Crane's observation of life in the slums, as did surely Jacob Riis's *How the Other Half Lives* (1890), a classic description of tenement life which Crane doubtless knew. He had heard this gifted journalist lecture on New York slums at the Seaside Assembly and perhaps had even met him, since he mentioned Riis in one of his *Tribune* reports.

Sometimes Lawrence accompanied Crane in his explorations of the mean side streets around Avenue A and the Bowery, the infamous mile-long street which cut through the immigrant districts of the Lower East Side where swarms of Jews, Italians, and Irish burrowed in the warrenlike rooms of massive tenement houses. They studied the jumble of humanity in notorious Mulberry Bend and Hester Street and the derelicts who crowded into Bowery saloons and ten-cent cot houses. In the evenings they were often at beer halls like the Atlantic Garden or Blank's near 14th Street or at one of the music halls like Koster and Bial's on 23rd Street, which was probably the model for the music hall Pete takes Maggie to in the novel.

One day, Lawrence remembered, Crane came in from one of his excursions in high excitement. "Did you ever see a stone-fight?" he asked, and launched into a graphic description of one he had just seen somewhere out in the tenements. "A little later that same day," Lawrence wrote, "the description had been set down on paper, and the first chapter of *Maggie* was written." In the weeks that followed, he filled page after page, writing for hours between rambles in the slums. "For a long time," Lawrence recalled, "he would sit wrapt in thought, devising his next sentence. Not until it had been completely formulated would he put pen to paper. Then he wrote slowly, carefully, in that legible round hand, with every punctuation mark accentuated, that always characterized his manuscripts. Rarely if ever did a word or mark require correction. That sentence completed, he would rise, relight his pipe, ramble around the room or look fixedly out of the windows. Usually he remained silent, wrapt in deep thought, but sometimes he would break into some popular song or bacchanalian ditty or sing a single bar of it over and over again while he waited for his inspiration to come."[1] Sometimes he worked a whole day over a single page and seldom wrote more than two or three.

Free-lance writing, he discovered, was a precarious business. Editors, bound by the conventions of routine daily journalism, showed little interest

Mulberry Bend, lower East Side New York, 1899 (courtesy The
New York Historical Society)

Crane at Pendennis Club, New York, probably in the spring of 1893 (courtesy Syracuse University)

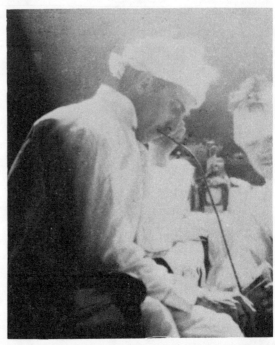

Cooper Square and the Bowery, New York, c. 1891 (courtesy The New York Historical Society)

TOP: *The Bowery, north from Grand Street, New York, 1896*
(courtesy The New York Historical Society)

Steve Brodie's Saloon, 114 Bowery, c. 1890 (courtesy The New
York Historical Society)

in colorful descriptions of New York street life like the unpublished piece about the injured street sweeper on 23rd Street who "flattened his face toward heaven and sent up a jet of violet, fastidious curses,"[2] or his impressionistic interview with an alderman under charges of corruption who "sat like a rural soup tureen in his chair and said 'Aw!' sadly whenever ash from his cigar bounced on his vest of blood and black."[3] How he lived is not altogether clear. He borrowed as freely as he could from friends and his brothers Ed and Will and went ill-clothed and sometimes hungry. "I was foolishly proud back then," he wrote later. "I hated to borrow money from my brothers who were not too well off. I borrowed too much which I have never paid back. The sane thing would have been simply to have lived with Will or Ed constantly and trusted to fortune for some luck in paying them back. They never asked me for a cent and that hurts like hellfire."[4] Wilbur's daughter Helen remembered that he would show up unexpectedly, smelling of tobacco and garlic, and stay until he tired of reproaches for "fooling away his time on the East Side with that driftwood of humanity. . . . He never had a clean shirt . . . and most of the time his toes were coming through his shoes 'most lamentably,' as he expressed it. His old gray ulster would have made quite a satisfactory stable-mop, but was scarcely good for anything else."[5]

Foolish as his voluntary experiment in misery might have seemed to him later, he looked on it at that time as a necessary part of his literary program. "I decided that the nearer a writer gets to life the greater he becomes as an artist," he wrote later. Literature, he had learned from Garland and Howells, ought to be grounded in real-life experience, and he had found in Kipling's *The Light That Failed* a striking dramatization of a realist artist's dogged pursuit of experience in its most crucial and challenging forms. Dick Heldar, the painter-hero of the novel, believes that his bitter sojourn in the slums of London revealed to him the quintessential human condition. "I never knew what I had to learn about the human face before," he says. When at last he sells one of his paintings, he calls on a friend to explain why he did not ask for help during his six months' ordeal: "I had a sort of superstition that this temporary starvation—that's what it was, and it hurt—would bring me more luck later."[6] Crane's life in the slums, though not likely consciously modeled on Heldar's, was remarkably like it, and like Heldar's was based on the belief that physical hardship is a necessary stimulus to art. "It was during this period that I wrote 'The Red

Badge of Courage.' It was an effort born of pain—despair, almost; and I believe that this made it a better piece of literature than it otherwise would have been."[7] But *The Red Badge* was still months away in the winter of 1892. He was at Ed's house in Lake View for Christmas, working on what he then called "A Girl of the Streets." It was apparently finished, or nearly so, when he returned to the city in January.

Louis Senger of Port Jervis, one of his camping friends who appears as "the tall man" in the Sullivan County sketches, called on him at the Pendennis Club in early January. The casual disorder of life in the old house made Senger uneasy, and Crane's medical student friends struck him as "a crowd of irresponsibles," too recklessly Bohemian for one whose sense of propriety had been permanently shaped by Port Jervis respectability. But Senger was sharply aware of Crane's genius for seeing "the ordinary and familiar with first eyes," and he read the manuscript of "A Girl of the Streets" with a true sense of its importance.

Senger's cousin, Corwin Knapp Linson, an artist and illustrator, had a studio in an ancient red brick building on the corner of Broadway and Thirtieth Street. Knowing Crane's interest in painting, Senger took him to meet Linson one snowy January afternoon. The painter knew all about Port Jervis, where he had once maintained a studio, and remembered vividly the rugged beauty of Sullivan County. Linson could talk interestingly about painting and painters; and Crane, who had heard lectures on art at the Seaside Assembly and perhaps Garland's enthusiastic talk about Impressionism, was prepared to take in his new friend's ideas. Linson recalled that Crane disapproved at this time of Impressionism, considering it affected and dishonest; but he later acknowledged its powers, most notably in a passage in his 1899 "War Memories," where he memorably described the revelatory effect of "mental light and shade" in the paintings of the French Impressionists.[8] Through Linson he got to know other artists and illustrators, dedicated young aesthetes living the romantically impoverished life of the studio that George du Maurier had described charmingly in his wildly popular *Trilby*. These enthusiastic Bohemians were contemplating styles and aesthetic ideas that neither Howells nor Garland would have had much sympathy for, ideas born of the free artistic life, touched by the spirit of Aubrey Beardsley and the fantastic Baudelaire, whose startling "The Buffoon and the Venus" Crane would soon imitate in his "A naked woman and a dead dwarf."[9] As Linson wrote, the watchword of the studios in those days was "style," which "came near to being worshiped as the end of art...."[10]

These ideas affected Crane chiefly by encouraging him to follow his natural inclinations. His literary ideas, as Linson reported them, seem much less radical than his actual style. He believed, as he told Linson, that narratives should be logical in action and faithful to character, and he believed in simplicity because he thought simplicity was truth. He detested the conventional language of popular literature. One day, Linson recalled, he flung a magazine to the floor in disgust, declaring that "any writer who will use such a mildewed phrase as 'from time immemorial' ought to have his brain sluiced."[11] Unusual images, odd conceits, quaint similes, sharply turned phrases were not so much conscious "style" as simply expressions of his characteristic way of seeing things.

That stormy winter, as blizzard followed blizzard and the city lay smothered in thick snow, Crane was often at Linson's gloomy studio, lounging on a ragged couch covered with a rumpled blanket and surrounded by piles of old magazines and papers and dirty canvases. He was tinkering with *Maggie*, revising it in light of advice from Will and some of his friends. Will had complained that the absence of names for the characters—they were simply epithets like "the girl," "the mere boy," "the woman of brilliance and audacity"—was confusing. He suggested the change in the title and, incidentally, advised Crane to get it copyrighted. Wallis McHarg, a friend from boyhood days in Asbury Park, visiting on his way to Germany to study medicine, had read it with grave misgivings. It was a doubtful subject for literature, he had thought, and like Will he had objected to the anonymity of the characters.

By late February or early March the novel was ready, and he began showing it to editors. Willis Johnson of the *Tribune* was impressed by "the throbbing vitality and dynamics of the story" but warned him that it would be hard to find a reputable publisher since it would obviously "shock the Podsnaps and Mrs. Grundys" and "bring on him a storm of condemnation."[12] What other editors said is not known, but Johnson's view was undoubtedly typical, and Crane wasted little time trying to find a publisher after these first efforts. Impatient to see it in print, he sold stock in a Pennsylvania coal mine he had inherited from his mother, borrowed money from William, and ordered 1,100 copies of the book from a lower Sixth Avenue print shop. Johnson's warning had convinced Crane, as he wrote later, that it would be better to publish under a pseudonym, and he asked a friend, "what he thought was the stupidest name in the world." The friend suggested "Johnson or Smith and 'Johnston Smith' went on the ugly yellow cover of the book by mistake. You see, I was going to wait until all the world was pyrotechnic about Johnston Smith's 'Maggie' and then I was going to flop down like a trapeze performer from the wire and, coming forward with all the modest grace of a consumptive nun, say, I am he, friends!..." The printing bill was $869, and he learned later that the print shop, which specialized in religious and medical books, overcharged him by about $700. "You may take this," he wrote someone, "as proffered evidence of my imbecility."[13]

The banal plot of the novel he was so eager to get before the public made *Maggie* more suitable, as it seems in broad outline, to sentimental melodrama than to literary art. It tells the story of Maggie Johnson, a young girl victimized by poverty and the viciousness of slum life. Her mother is the Amazonian Mary Johnson, well known in police courts for her frequent drunken rampages. She alternately beats her children and smothers them with maudlin demonstrations of affection. The brooding, indifferent father protests the beatings because they disturb his peace. The sickly baby, Tommie, dies of abuse and neglect. Jimmie, Maggie's younger brother, grows up to become a truck driver who bullies the world from the high seat of his van, bawling curses and threats at pedestrians and other drivers. He lounges on street corners with Pete, a swaggering bartender who at sixteen wears the "chronic sneer of an ideal manhood." Jimmie introduces Pete to the blossoming Maggie, who sees in the bartender a fascinating man of the world, admirable for the awesome power of his fists and his masterful knowledge of the ways of the streets. The mother accuses Maggie of yielding to Pete's sexual advances and drives her out of the tenement, outraged, as is Jimmie, by her affront to their respectability. Maggie accepts Pete's protection, but he quickly tires of her, and when he turns her out, she drifts into prostitution. One evening, in a mood of despair, she turns away from the bright avenue where she plies her trade, makes her way through dark streets to the river, and drowns herself. When Jimmie brings the news to their mother, she bawls tearfully to the assembled women of the tenement, "Oh yes, I'll fergive her! I'll fergive her!"

As the novelist Frank Norris pointed out three years later, this was an old story by the time Crane came to tell it. He "strikes no new note," Norris

Price, 50 Cents

MAGGIE

A Girl of the Streets

(A STORY OF NEW YORK)

By

JOHNSTON SMITH

Copyrighted

Cover of the first edition of Maggie: A Girl of the Streets, *1893* (courtesy Barrett Collection, University of Virginia)

Crane on the couch in Corwin Knapp Linson's New York studio, c. 1893 (courtesy Syracuse University)

wrote. "Most of his characters are old acquaintances in the world of fiction and we know all about—or, at least, certain novelists have pretended to tell us all about the life of the mean streets of a great city. In ordinary hands the tale of 'Maggie' would be 'twice told.' "[14] And it would have been. In the eighties and early nineties reformers and philanthropists like T. D. Talmage, J. W. Buel, and Jacob Riis had created a stereotype of the pure and virtuous slum girl and her struggle against the powers of her brutal world. Though sometimes able, according to this popular myth, to resist these powers through sheer strength of character, she was often driven to prostitution, despair, and suicide. Frequently identified as cause of these tragedies was the cruel indifference of society at large and the hypocrisy and moral obtuseness of those clergymen and "respectable" people who condemned and cast them aside. "There is not one person out of a thousand," Talmage wrote, "that will . . . come so near to the heart of the Lord Jesus Christ as to dare to help one of these fallen souls."[15] B. O. Flower, a close observer of this life, wrote a series of editorials in his radical magazine, the *Arena*, describing the sad plight of "poor factory and sewing girls, whose fate is often so grimly tragic that it is only their splendid moral strength which keeps them from the abyss of vice."[16] About the time Crane was drafting his first story of a prostitute in the spring of 1891 at Syracuse University, the *Arena* published several articles explaining the effect of the slums on the morals of its inhabitants, citing the saloon as the chief cause of its miseries and condemning public hypocrisy and the sham of respectability as bars to constructive reformist action. "We are in the midst of an era of sham," one writer noted. "We do not care so much that vice exists as that it be well-dressed."[17]

The plot of *Maggie* is a fabrication of elements drawn from this familiar pattern of themes, ideas, and attitudes. The characters (the pure, betrayed Maggie who "blossomed in a mud puddle" only to fall victim to her heartless seducer, drunken parents, and vicious brother), the attitudes (the author's scorn of "respectable" people, his assumption of Maggie's essential innocence), the action (the fights, the suicide), and the attribution of causes (alcohol, social determinism, the hypocrisy of the respectable world) are the basic elements of the stereotypical plot. Edgar Fawcett had used the plot in his 1889 novel of the slums, *The Evil That Men Do*, more than two years before Crane began *Maggie*. Cora Stang, the heroine in Fawcett's novel, is "a delicate blushing-rose in the midst of . . . smirk and soilure," and though she aspires to be "a flower of sinless and beautiful love," she is seduced and abandoned, victimized by "the savage forces of birth, heredity, and poverty." She is scorned by respectable people of "egoistic indifference" who "murder philanthropy," and her brief career as a prostitute ends tragically in her murder.

What saves *Maggie* from the inherent banality of the well-known story is Crane's treatment. The "phrase-by-phrase concentration, the steady brilliance, and the large design," as John Berryman says, reflect the conception of art that "initiated modern American writing."[18] In method, he is radically new. He casts aside the familiar devices and conventions of fiction; he abandons customary narrative order and tells the story in a series of loosely related episodes. He makes few concessions to literal realism, presenting the tenement world in a constant flurry of images that seem to refer less to its objective reality than to its effect on the feelings and ideas of the characters. A looming tenement house is displaced in time and space, seen dreamlike with its "hundred windows" and "dozen gruesome doorways" that give up "loads of babies to the street and gutter" while "withered persons . . . sat smoking pipes in obscure corners."[19] The short, simple sentences abound in odd turns of phrases, unexpected metaphors, revelations of strange perspectives. A saloon squats on a corner, its open mouth calling seductively. All things seem to be projections of someone's hopes, desires, and fears. Walking the avenue, Maggie the prostitute encounters "a stout gentleman, with pompous and philanthropic whiskers, who went stolidly by, the broad of his back sneering at the girl." "The picture he makes," Norris wrote perceptively, "is not a single carefully composed painting, serious, finished, scrupulously studied, but rather scores and scores of tiny flashlight photographs, instantaneous, caught, as it were, on the run."[20] *Maggie* is hardly an example of social realism, despite Crane's declared allegiance to the doctrines of Howells and Garland. Deeply indebted as it was to commonplace social myths, it seemed altogether innovative, as Garland acknowledged when he wrote later that Crane "had the genius which makes an old world new."[21]

Crane sent a copy anonymously to Garland, who happened to be visiting in New York from Boston about the time it came from the printer. Recognizing the "vividness and originality of the writing" as Crane's, perhaps from his memory of the Asbury Park parade story and the Sullivan County sketches, he asked Crane to call. Garland saw in *Maggie* the kind

of writing he would shortly describe in his antitraditional book on literature and the arts, *Crumbling Idols* (1894). He strongly encouraged the
young writer and with characteristic energy set about bringing him to the
attention of editors and literary men like Flower of the *Arena*, S. S. Mc-
Clure of the McClure Syndicate, and William Dean Howells, one of the
most powerful literary men in the country. On Garland's advice, Crane
sent Howells a copy of *Maggie*, and Garland prepared Howells for it by
describing it to him over lunch.

With Garland and Howells as allies Crane could have expected a
critical success, but on the very day Garland was praising him to Howells,
he received a letter from John D. Barry, editor of the *Forum*, which expressed succinctly the prevailing literary prejudices against which *Maggie*
would have to make its way. "It is pitilessly real," Barry wrote Crane, "and
it produced its effect upon me—the effect, I presume, that you wished to
produce, a kind of horror. To be frank with you, I doubt if such literature
is good: it closely approaches the morbid and the morbid is always dangerous." The effect of illuminating reality that Garland admired was less
important to Barry than its impact on the reader's taste and sensibility. "I
know one might say that the truth was black and that you tried to describe
it just as it was; but, one ought always to bear in mind that literature is an
art, that effect, the effect upon the reader, must always be kept in view by
the artist and as soon as that effect approaches the morbid, the unhealth-
ful, the art becomes diseased." No such literature, Barry wrote, can fulfill
its proper aim, which is to inspire improving thought and action. "I presume you wish to make people think about the horrible things you describe. But of what avail is their thought unless it leads them to work? It
would be better for them not to think about these things at all—if thinking
ends as it began, for in itself it is unpleasant and in its tendency un-
healthful."[22] Barry's letter "touched Steve for its proof of genuine interest,"[23] Linson recalled, but its argument, as Crane must have sadly felt,
belonged to the world of his elders, to a literary tradition he had not even
bothered to learn before rejecting it. It was a clear warning of what to
expect. "This work is a mudpuddle, I am told on the best authority," he
wrote in a copy he sent to a friend. "Wade in and have a swim."[24] He
inscribed a copy to a certain Miss Wortzmann in words that seem to
comment on Barry's: "This story will not edify or improve you and may not
even interest you but I owe your papa $1.30 for tobacco."[25]

Howells's response, however, was more encouraging than Barry's. The critic was slow getting around to *Maggie*, and Crane wrote him after a time a plaintive note saying that he had decided, having heard nothing from him, that Howells had found it "a wretched thing."[26] Howells then read it and, finding that he in fact "cared for it immensely," invited Crane to call on him. He struck Howells as a young man of immense power who had not yet come to his full expression. He recalled years later that Crane spoke "wisely and kindly" about the poor and that he seemed notably indifferent to the theories of reformers.[27] Howells used his influence with bookstores to try to get them to stock *Maggie* and advised Crane to send copies to certain ministers he knew to be interested in slum conditions ("maniacs for reform," Crane called them). But Brentano's bookstore, which took twelve copies, returned ten; and a Catholic notable wrote Crane that the book was an insult to the Irish. "I shall never understand," Howells said years later, "what was found offensive in the little tragedy."[28]

But Crane's confidence, sustained by the admiration of two famous literary men, was unshaken. "Well, at least, I've done something," he wrote Lily euphorically. "I wrote a book. . . . Hamlin Garland was the first to overwhelm me with all manner of extraordinary language. The book has made me a powerful friend in W. D. Howells." He was now known and admired, he said, by editors like B. O. Flower of the *Arena*, the editor of the *Review of Reviews*, and even the editor of the *Forum*, John Barry, who had severely criticized *Maggie* in late March. "So I think I can say that if I 'watch out,' I'm almost a success. And 'such a boy, too,' they say."[29] Linson recalled that he talked much about Howells and Garland, basking and expanding in the glow of their praise, and Willis Johnson remembered even after thirty years the "illumination of countenance and exaltation of spirit which he displayed when he came to tell me of his interviews with them."[30]

But his euphoria was short-lived. Within a few weeks it was clear that *Maggie* would not make his literary fame and fortune. "My first great disappointment was in the reception of 'Maggie, a Girl of the Streets' " he wrote. "I remember how I looked forward to its publication, and pictured the sensation I thought it would make. It fell flat. Nobody seemed to notice it or care for it. . . . Poor Maggie! she was one of my first loves."[31] He hoped for a while that he might catch the attention of some willing regular publisher, but it was a forlorn hope. *Maggie*, it appeared, was dead. According to legend, Jennie Creegan, the Pendennis Club housemaid, used some of the volumes stacked along the walls in Crane's and Lawrence's room to fire the stove.

Crane was no better off materially, of course, than in the terrible winter of 1892. Editors were willing to take an occasional special article, but it was as hard as ever to live on the precarious income from these uncertain sales. What little money he managed to get always "slipped through his fingers without leaving a trace."[32] A few unbearable days as a clerk in a men's clothing store on Bleecker Street gave him the idea for "Why Did the Young Clerk Swear," a trifle about the comical irritation of a young clerk whose customers constantly interrupt his reading of a torrid French romance.[33] He spent all of the fifteen dollars he got for it in one night—on a champagne supper.

In February or March of 1893 he had begun rummaging through Linson's copies of the *Century* magazine's *Battles and Leaders of the Civil War*, storing up ideas for a war story he had in mind, originally conceived as "a potboiler," he told Louis Senger, "something that would take the boarding-school element. . . ."[34] He also borrowed copies of the *Century* from a Mrs. Armstrong, a woman he had known as a child in Asbury Park. According to legend, she had once spanked him for burying a small boy in the sand on the beach while playing war and then digging him up (as he explained to the inquiring lady when she caught him in the act) to retrieve the canteen of "whiskey" he had forgotten to take off the "corpse." But he returned Mrs. Armstrong's magazines in early April. "I have spent ten nights writing a story of the war on my own responsibility," he said in a note, "but I am not sure that my facts are real and the books won't tell me what I want to know so I must do it all over again, I guess."[35] These matter-of-fact accounts by veterans of the War irritated him. "I wonder that *some* of these fellows don't tell how they *felt* in those scraps!" he scolded impatiently to Linson. "They spout eternally of what they *did*, but they are as emotionless as rocks!"[36] It was not the facts of war he was after; these he knew from his lifelong fascination with battles and soldiering. His search was for the problematic relationship between feeling and fact as revealed by a mind under the stress of supreme crisis. It was Tolstoy, he would come to realize, who would give him a model for this perspective on war, not the ex-soldiers in their pedestrian personal histories in the *Century*.

About mid-April the Pendennis Club disbanded, and when Mrs. Blanchard, the "dragon" landlady, took over a boarding house on 15th Street, Crane joined her there. But he also spent much time at Linson's and the studios of several artists and illustrators living in the old Art Students League building on East 23rd Street, a massive, gloomy structure so intricate in its meandering halls and oddly situated rooms "that it took an expert pilot to guide a stranger through its mysteries." Its upper floors were occupied by "artists, musicians and writers, young men and women, decent people all, who were glad of the low rents and really congenial atmosphere," one of the artists, Frederic Gordon, wrote. A line from Emerson chalked on an old beam in a remote upper studio seemed appropriate to the Bohemian spirit of the place: "Congratulate yourselves if you have done something strange and extravagant and broken the monotony of a decorous age."[37] Among these free-spirited artists at various times were Gordon, David Ericson, Nelson Greene, and R. G. Vosburgh. Ericson remembered that Crane worked some on the war story there that spring. "I remember one time when he was lying in a hammock of his saying 'That is great!' It shocked me for a moment. I thought how conceited he is. But when he read me the passage, I realized at once how wonderfully real it was. . . ."[38] He was still composing it when he moved into the Art Students League building in the fall and, as Ericson recalled, was still consulting Linson's copies of the *Century*.

But he was also concentrating that spring on pieces he thought he might sell to the magazines. He turned to the Johnsons' tenement world again for three stories about the baby Tommie, who dies in chapter four of the novel and is carried away in an "insignificant coffin, his small waxen hand clutching a flower that the girl, Maggie, had stolen from an Italian."[39] In the anecdotal "A Great Mistake" the urchin attempts to steal fruit from an Italian's pushcart, but the alert vendor catches him in the act and pries open his tiny hand to retrieve a lemon.[40] "A Dark Brown Dog" is a perfectly detached account of senseless cruelty to an affectionate puppy Tommie finds in the street.[41] Although the child periodically beats the adoring dog with a stick, the two become fast friends, sharing together the hazard of being small creatures in the violence of the Johnsons' apartment. "An Ominous Baby" tells how Tommie wanders into a rich neighborhood, seizes a splendid red toy fire engine from a little boy, and flees with it, "weeping with the air of a wronged one who has at last succeeded in achieving his rights."[42] The story dramatizes the division between the haves and have nots, in which Crane saw a potential for "ominous" class strife, but it touches also on an idea that recurs often in his writing—his conviction that primitive desire and irrepressible self-assertion are ultimate motives in human nature. The young child as pure ego, as candid and unabashed aggressor, appears often in his work, representing primitive forces in nature powerfully resistant to constraints of human law and social conventions.

Crane wrote a farcical story about the embarrassing adventures of two men at the beach who doze on a raft and are carried out to sea in ridiculous bathing suits. Linson agreed to do illustrations for the story on spec. Crane and the painter went out on the red tin roof of Linson's studio with a photographer to pose under a broiling sun as the two derelicts, and Crane shouted at the camera, "Hurry up there. Gosh! You can brown wheats on this tin."[43] Nothing came of their project. A careless editor lost Linson's illustrations, and the story was not published until 1900, five months before Crane died.

In June he went to Ed's in Lake View to work on the war novel, about the time Garland's review of *Maggie* appeared in the *Arena*. Garland praised the novel for its "astonishingly good style. . . . It is pictorial, graphic, terrible in its directness. It has no conventional phrases." But he ended with a disclaimer which shows that, despite his vaunted iconoclasm, he had not altogether vanquished certain sentimental literary notions of the age. "The story fails of rounded completeness. It is only a fragment. It is typical only of the worst elements of the alley. The author should delineate the families living on the next street, who live lives of heroic purity and hopeless hardship."[44] It was about this time, in the spring or early summer, that Crane conceived the idea for his novel *George's Mother*, in which he shows a more "normal" life of the slums in his story of the courageous and spirited Mrs. Kelcey, who lives with her worthless son George in the same tenement house occupied by the vicious Johnsons. Although the view Crane takes of the Kelceys is probably not what Garland had in mind, the critic may have suggested, when they talked about writing in March, the idea of a companion piece to *Maggie* showing a more hopeful side of slum life.

At Ed's house in Lake View he played football and worked on the war novel. Part of the summer he spent in Port Jervis with William and Wilbur

and in camp in Pennsylvania. In the fall he was back at the Art Students'
League building with Gordon, Ericson, and Vosburgh, writing and rewriting the war story all that fall and winter, working usually in the quiet night
from midnight until four or five in the morning and sleeping most of the
day. Linson said the old building was a maze which "housed various developing ambitions as a hive holds bees. . . . The furniture supported the
clutter of drawings, ink bottles, tobacco, bread, pipes, unwashed cups, and
various garments. Tumbled cots and crippled chairs filled spaces not taken
by battered trunks and a stove. . . ."[45] Vosburgh, Linson, and others recalled
the winter of 1893, the lowest point of the worst economic depression in
the history of the country before the nineteen thirties, as a time of "direst
poverty" at the Art Students League. For days, Linson said, Crane's only
food was the "free lunch" at a saloon on the corner. The artists sometimes
painted on towels because they had no money for canvas, and on bitter
cold days they stayed in bed to keep warm because they could not buy fuel
for the stove.

Garland was in New York that winter, sharing an apartment on 105th
Street with his brother Franklin, an actor who was appearing in James A.
Herne's *Shore Acres* at Daly's Theatre. One day in March, Crane appeared
at the Garlands' apartment, pale and thin, wearing the familiar old gray
ulster, smoking nervously. He seemed depressed, but as he warmed under
the influence of Franklin's steak and coffee he "talked freely and well,
always with precision and original tang." He suddenly drew a roll of
manuscript from his pocket and held it out to Garland. Garland unrolled
the sheets and found they contained a number of poems. He was startled
and delighted to read in Crane's clear youthful script the poem "God fash-
ioned the ship of the world carefully," which goes on to relate how God, in
a heedless moment, let the craft slip away unfinished to drift rudderless
forever, "going ridiculous voyages" and inspiring much mirth among the
angels.[46] The critic read the other poems while Crane waited. "I could not
believe they were the work of the pale reticent boy moving restlessly about
the room," he wrote. Crane said he had been writing five or six a day and
had at that very moment "five or six all in a little row up here," pointing to
his temple. He came the next day with another half dozen and told Garland he had "three more waiting in line." At the critic's urging, he sat down
and produced "one of his most powerful verses. It flowed from his pen like
oil. . . ."[47] Crane had already shown them to Linson, who had told him
that their value was in "their newness of form, their disregard of the

usual," though he had frankly admitted that he could not always understand them. "That's all right, CK," Crane had replied. "If you can see them
like that it's all I want."[48]

More than half of these poems, most of them written before the end of
April and published the next year as *The Black Riders*, are on religious
themes: the inscrutability of God, man's futile quest for God, God's wrath,
the terrors of a Godless universe, man's pride and impotence. The old
issues about man and God harangued from the Methodist pulpits of
Stephen's early childhood obviously lingered on, troublesome now in the
context of his skepticism. Is God dead and man abandoned to an indifferent universe, the questioning runs, or is He still awfully present, a God of
wrath breathing hatred and malice on helpless, sinful men? In some poems
God appears as a poignant vision of kindliness and compassion; in others
He is cold, remote, removed to impossible distances. The mood from poem
to poem alternates between blasphemy and piety. "Well, I hate Thee,
unrighteous picture," the speaker of one rails against the God of wrath who
decrees that the sins of fathers shall be visited on the heads of the children:

> Wicked image, I hate Thee;
> So, strike with Thy vengeance
> The heads of those little men
> Who come blindly.
> It will be a brave thing.[49]

In one poem a man is certain that the mighty boom of thunder is the voice
of God, but the idea is disputed:

> "Not so," said a man.
> "The voice of God whispers in the heart
> So softly
> That the soul pauses. . . ."[50]

The speaker agonizes over the thought that in "the mighty sky" is naught
but "a vast blue, / Echoless, ignorant—."[51] The God of wrath and the God
of indifference are often suggested by contrasting images of hostile or im-
perturbable mountains. In one poem, a range of angry mountains appears
as a vengeful army threatening a defiant little man:

Crane and Linson on the roof of Linson's studio, 1894 (courtesy
Syracuse University)

Crane and Linson seated on the roof of Linson's studio, 1894 (courtesy Syracuse University)

Crane and Lucius Button, a Pendennis Club medical student, on the roof of Linson's studio at 42 West 30th Street, New York, 1894 (courtesy Syracuse University)

On the horizon the peaks assembled;
And as I looked,
The march of the mountains began.
As they marched, they sang,
"Aye! We come! We come!"[52]

And in another:

Once I saw mountains angry,
And ranged in battle-front.
Against them stood a little man;
Aye, he was no bigger than my finger.[53]

Another man, "clambering to the house-tops" to appeal to the heavens, finds God at last, in "the sky . . . filled with armies."[54]

Clearly, there was a side to this laconic, skeptical young man, who seemed so unorthodox in thought and feeling, that even his close friends did not know. The imagery in the Sullivan County sketches of violent or forbiddingly indifferent nature, as the poems in *The Black Riders* amply confirm, derives obviously from his heritage as a minister's son. Bishop Peck's adjurations in *What Must I Do to Be Saved?* clearly lingered in his imagination as an ominous threat in a fallen world where bewildered little men are ruled by fear and futile longing.

Crane's raucous friends at the Art Students' League ("Indians," as he called them) taunted him about his "lines," which they found deeply puzzling, being accustomed to rhyming poems in regular meter on well-established "poetic" subjects. "They think I'm a joke, the Indians!" he told Linson with a grin and showed him a satirical squib he found pinned on the wall with a caricature of his distinctive profile.[55] But John Barry, the editor who had cautioned him about the shocking *Maggie*, greatly admired them. He arranged for Crane to appear at a formal, full dress literary affair at Sherry's in honor of Mrs. Frances Hodgson Burnett, creator of *Little Lord Fauntleroy*, where she and several of her guests were to read from their works. Crane refused to appear as either reader or guest, declaring that he "would rather die than do it,"[56] and Barry undertook to read several of the poems himself, after which a crowd of the poet's friends, some of whom had come from Port Jervis for the occasion, led the applause. Linson recalled that Crane waited anxiously at the studio. "A glowing report sent Steve to bed happy, but to convince him took some effort."[57]

While he was writing *Maggie, The Red Badge,* and *The Black Riders,* Crane continued his explorations of the Bowery and tenement districts, sometimes disappearing for days and returning to someone's studio exhausted and ill, looking himself like one of the derelicts whose way of life he was studying. These experiences produced more than a dozen sketches and stories of street life; two, the vivid "An Experiment in Misery,"[58] and "The Men in the Storm,"[59] are notable innovations in the art of description. In "An Experiment in Misery" the imagery of torpor and disease in the packed, odorous common room of a cot house (like "a graveyard, where bodies were merely flung"), the oblique evocation of violence and wounding in the "scar-like impressions" the trampling mob leaves in the spattered black mud on the sidewalk, and the sense of foreboding in the image of an elevated train as "some monstrous kind of crab squatting over the street" suggest unforgettably "a red and grim tragedy of the unfathomable possibilities" of suffering. As Crane depicts it, it is indeed a world of grinding, granite wheels, and yet the feckless young derelict who tells the writer without shame how his father and a succession of employers had turned him out as a drunkard and shirker exemplifies an incorrigible personal irresponsibility which Crane balances aganst evidences of cruel and invincible social forces. "In a story of mine called 'An Experiment in Misery,' " he wrote to a young woman who criticized him for his indifference in *Maggie* to reform, "I tried to make plain that the root of Bowery life is a sort of cowardice. Perhaps I mean a lack of ambition or to willingly be knocked flat and accept the licking."[60] In "The Men in the Storm" he explicitly distinguishes between men of "patience, industry, and temperance," who are merely down on their luck, and the shiftless denizens of the Bowery.

Some time in April, Crane moved out of the League building to a room on West 33rd Street, where, as he wrote Garland, "People can come to see me now. They come in sho[a]ls and say that I am a great writer." Though he sold articles occasionally to the *Press,* his financial condition had not much improved. He explained to Garland that he had not been to see him "because of various strange conditions—notably, my toes are coming through one shoe and I have not been going out into society as much as I might."[61] Linson called one day to see why he had not been to the studio and found him virtually a prisoner in his room because he had no shoes. The artist left and returned shortly to present him a new pair. Thus released from his confinement, he soon appeared at Garland's apartment, bearing another manuscript.

It was the first part of "Private Fleming, His Various Battles," later retitled *The Red Badge of Courage*. What struck Garland as he read eagerly through the first seven or eight chapters was the power of Crane's imagination. "The first sentence fairly took me captive," he wrote. "It described a vast army in camp on one side of a river, confronting with its thousands of eyes a similar monster on the opposite bank. The finality which lay in every word, the epic breadth of vision, the splendor of the pictures presented—all indicated a most powerful and original imagination. . . ."[62] He saw clearly that it was Crane's genius for evoking theme and idea in such imagery that transformed the commonplace conventions of the Civil War story into literature. Once again, as he had in *Maggie*, Crane drew heavily on popular sources, in this case on the *Century* memoirs and such books as Wilbur Hinman's *Corporal Si Klegg and His Pard* (1887). In these he found the familiar elements of his plot: the young man who goes to war with his head full of heroic fantasies inspired by patriotic rhetoric and tales from the battlefield; the disapproval of wiser parents; his impatience with the apparent purposelessness of troop movements and incompetence of generals; the shattering of his illusions in his first battle; and similar standard motifs, incidents, and situations. But armed with an innovative style, drawn in some intricate way from Kipling, Tolstoy, and the Impressionist painters, Crane added new dimensions to the commonplace story. Like Tolstoy's powerful antiheroic novel of the Crimean War, *Sebastopol*, Crane's demonstrates the ironic effect of describing reality as subjective perception; like Kipling's *The Light That Failed*, Crane's novel makes special uses of color and other pictorial effects; and like Impressionist paintings, it conveys a feeling of reality in constant flux, changing as the mood or point of view of the observer changes from moment to moment.

The surreal distortion in the opening description of the landscape that Garland found so striking is characteristic of the hero's anxiety-directed perception. From the beginning Henry Fleming's psychological plight is dramatized in imagery that seems to equate war and nature. To his overwrought mind, the terror of war and the terror of nature are often indis-

First page of the manuscript of The Red Badge of Courage, *shown to Hamlin Garland and Irving Bacheller in early 1894 (courtesy Barrett Collection, University of Virginia)* tinguishable. Mountains, fields, streams, the night, the sun, appear in his disordered perception as living creatures, monstrous and fearsome. He sees the "red eye-like gleam of hostile camp-fires set in the low brows of distant hills" and the black columns of enemy troops disappearing on the brow of a hill "like two serpents crawling from the cavern of night." When his regiment, marching to the front, crosses a little stream, he fancies that the black water below the bridge looks at him with "white bubble-eyes"; he imagines "fierce-eyed hosts" lurking in the shadows of the woods. When he throws down his rifle and takes to his heels in his first battle, he flees not so much his Confederate enemy as the "onslaught of redoubtable dragons," of "red and green monsters" that seem to spring out of the very landscape. As such metaphors suggest, Henry is as anxious about how he measures up to nature (and, by extension, to God, as the symbolism of *The Black Riders* indicates) as he is about how he measures up to war.

The meaning of nature shifts as Henry's moods and fortunes shift. His fear is nature's hostility, his complacency is nature's sympathy. In his humiliation after his cowardly flight from battle, he looks desperately to nature for solace and comfort. Weaving his way through a peaceful forest, he comes to feel, conveniently, that nature is "a woman with a deep aversion to tragedy." He reaches a secluded place where "high, arching boughs made a chapel," a retreat, as he supposes, provided by a tender Mother Nature for his spiritual comfort. He pushes aside "green doors" and is suddenly transfixed with horror. Sitting on the "gentle brown carpet" in the "religious half-light" is a rotting corpse, an abomination in what he has taken to be a sacrosanct retreat in the very bosom of nature. As he bolts in terror, nature seems suddenly to turn on him in a fury; snagging branches and brambles seem to try to draw him back to the unspeakable corpse. But from a distance, nature seems once again peaceful and tender. "The trees about the portal of the chapel moved sighingly in a soft wind. A sad silence was upon the little, guarding edifice."[63]

Sometimes, when his consciousness is caught momentarily off guard, Henry seems to catch fleeting glimpses of objective reality and is astonished when he finds it at odds with his expectations. Once after a furious fight he glances upward and feels "a flash of astonishment at the blue, pure sky and the sun-gleamings on the trees and fields"; he finds it "surprising that nature had gone tranquilly on with her golden processes in the midst of so much devilment."[64] Such distortions measure Henry's moral vulnerability. Fear and vanity color and distort truth. He is never sure whether nature is hostile, or sympathetic, or merely indifferent, and not knowing, he has no way of fixing his place in the scheme of things.

These metaphors and images are signs of an underlying motive *The Red Badge* shares with *The Black Riders*; both books reflect the spiritual uneasiness Crane inevitably reveals in subject, theme, or image in most of his writings. But another feature of the novel is its persistent preoccupation with the heroic. Crane's sense of the heroic was formed in the conflict between his ironic skepticism and his pride in the deeds of his military ancestors. The resolution of that conflict left him ambivalent about heroism, at once reverential and derisive, but he seems finally to come to focus on the virtues of humility and selfless devotion to duty. When Henry rejoins his regiment with the assistance of the humble "cheery soldier," he discovers that the braggart Wilson, "the loud soldier," has undergone a remarkable change: he is no longer concerned with "the proportions of his personal prowess" but shows now a "fine reliance" and "quiet belief in his purposes and abilities." He is no longer "a loud, young soldier." Henry wonders "where had been born these new eyes" and reflects that Wilson apparently "had now climbed a peak of wisdom from which he could perceive himself as a very wee thing."[65] Having exorcised his corrupting vanity, Wilson sees himself and the world clearly and sanely. But Henry never does. Reflecting on his conduct at the end, as his regiment marches away from the field of battle, he seems one moment to be fully aware of the disabling effect of his vanity and self-complacency and the next once again enthralled by sentimental delusions and egotistical fantasies. But his self-congratulatory notion that his newfound wisdom has at last brought him into harmony with the universe is unmistakably undercut by Crane's irony, and at the end of the novel Henry is as vulnerable to self-serving illusions as ever. His plight, revealed in the sentimental image of "a golden ray of sun" breaking "through the hosts of lead rain clouds," measures the depth of Crane's skepticism.

In *The Red Badge* Crane tapped for the first time the full powers of his imagination. The pathos of Henry's alienation in an incomprehensible world, of his helplessness under the spell of his vanity, and of his poignant yearning for a sign is brilliantly realized and rendered. "I experienced the thrill of the editor who has fallen unexpectedly upon the work of a genius," Garland said when he first read it in manuscript.[66] Like the critic, the whole literary world would in time admire the splendor of Crane's depiction of the fantastic landscape, the humor of the scene in which the country maiden battles heroically to rescue her cow from the fat thieving soldier, the horror of Henry's discovery in the little forest chapel, the awesome death of Jim Conklin, the patient and selfless suffering of the mortally wounded "tattered man," the quiet competence and kindliness of the anonymous "cheery soldier," and the many other memorable scenes, incidents, and characters. The novel's psychological and symbolic truth is so compelling that few readers notice how vulnerable it is as a rendition of the literal facts of war. But in a sense *The Red Badge* is only incidentally about war, despite the fact that it is modelled nominally on the Battle of Chancellorsville. It is a drama of a mind under the stress of extreme crisis, and in this view a triumph of realism.

Garland gave Crane good advice about removing excessive dialect forms in the speech of the characters and lent him fifteen dollars to pay a typist who was holding the last half of the manuscript "in hock." Before the critic left New York in late April to take up permanent residence in Chicago, he gave Crane a letter recommending his work to S. S. McClure. In early May the writer took the revised novel, now titled *The Red Badge of Courage*, to the publisher, who seemed sure he could use it, either for distribution to his newspaper syndicate or as a serial in *McClure's Magazine*.

With publication of the novel assured, as he thought, Crane turned to other work. He wrote a Decoration Day piece for the *Press* in which he celebrated the "fidelity to truth and to duty" of the "brave, simple, quiet men," the veterans of the Union army, "who crowded upon the opposing bayonets of their country's enemies."[67] The *Press* rejected it as too intricate for its readers, but it printed "Billy Atkins Went to Omaha," a tale about a tramp who suffers terrible hardships riding the "blind side" of a baggage car from Denver to Omaha and back, for no reason except to be going somewhere—an experience notably "incoherent," Crane wrote, "like the detailed accounts of great battles."[68] But what occupied him chiefly this spring and summer was another novel of slum life, "A Woman Without Weapons" (later retitled *George's Mother*), begun in the spring of 1893, probably with Garland's encouragement, and laid aside for *The Red Badge of Courage*. Free at last of the war novel, he took up *George's Mother* again in high spirits. His *Press* articles were apparently bringing in enough, for once, to live on. He wrote Garland in May that he was eating "with charming regularity at least two times per day. I am content and am writing another novel which is a bird."[69]

At John Barry's suggestion he sent about seventy of his poems to Copeland and Day, Boston publishers of experimental poetry, and the editors shortly proposed to bring them out as a book. When he left the city for Port Jervis in late May, he had good reason to be pleased with the progress of his literary career, even though he had had no definite word from McClure as to when or in what form he would bring out *The Red Badge*. In June, McClure commissioned him and Linson to do an illustrated article on Pennsylvania coal mines for his magazine. Linson, who negotiated the assignment, was exasperated to find that the unpredictable Crane had departed without a word to anyone. The painter, eventually guessing his whereabouts, found him sitting contentedly on Louis Senger's front porch in Port Jervis. They proceeded to Scranton for a two-day tour of the mines, and Stephen, sitting at a window in his Valley House hotel room, wrote with incredible fluency, as Linson recalled, one of his best sketches, "In the Depths of a Coal Mine." The opening paragraph, a variant of the fantasy-like beginning of *The Red Badge*, describes the gigantic coal breakers squatting on the hills "like enormous preying monsters eating the sunshine, the grass, the green leaves."[70] His characteristic figures and images of monsters in the landscape, of mysterious hills, of a somber and vaguely forbidding countryside, and of the "sky of imperial blue, incredibly far away" over this sad and stricken land, are signs that his descent into the inferno-like mine stirred his deepest imagination, calling up those symbols of the fallen world and impossible ideals he had been developing since they first appeared, in other forms, in the Sullivan County sketches.

Linson returned to the city to get started on the coal mine illustrations, fourteen of which appeared with the article, and Crane stopped over in Port Jervis to work on *George's Mother* and get ready for the big annual Pennsylvania camping trip. He wrote Copeland and Day from his camp in Pike County for word about *The Black Riders*, but the publishers' response was not reassuring; they wanted to leave out certain poems, particularly the blasphemous poems about God, and they asked for new ones to replace them. From Hartwood, a village near Port Jervis where his brother Ed now lived, Crane replied belligerently: "I should absolutely refuse to have my poems printed without many of those which you just as

Draft page of "In the Depths of a Coal Mine," 1894 (courtesy Barrett Collection, University of Virginia)

Original Mss. by Stephen Crane.
written in the Valley House, at Scranton, Pa

First draft of "In the depths of a Coal mine". McClure's—aug. 1894

The "breakers" squatted upon the hillsides and in the valley like enormous preying monsters eating of the sunshine, the grass, the green leaves. The smoke and dust from their nostrils had devastated the atmosphere. All that remained of the ~~grass~~ vegetation looked dark, miserable, half-strangled. Along the summit-line of the mountain, a few unhappy trees were etched upon the clouds. Overhead stretched a sky of imperial blue, incredibly faraway from the sombre land.

We approached our first colliery over paths of coal-dust that wound among the switches. ~~around and~~ The "breaker" loomed ~~high~~ above us, a huge and towering building of blackened wood. It quaintly resembled some extravagant Swiss chalet. It ended in a little curious peak and upon its side there was a profusion of windows appearing at strange and unexpected points. Through occasional doors one could see the flash of whirring machinery. Men with wondrously blackened faces sometimes came forth from it. The sole glitter upon their persons was at their hats where the little tin lamps were carried. They went stolidly along, some

Crane and Linson at the Scranton coal mine that Crane studied for his article in McClure's Magazine, *1894 (courtesy Syracuse University)*

absolutely mark 'No.' It seems to me that you cut all the ethical sense out of the book. All the anarchy, perhaps. It is the anarchy which I particularly insist upon. . . . The [poems] which refer to God, I believe you condemn altogether. I am obliged to have them in when my book is printed." He would write no more poems for the book, he added. "We would be obliged to come to an agreement upon those that are written."[71] The publishers responded with a list of seven they wanted to omit, two of them about God, and hinted that they might reject the whole lot if Crane refused the compromise. The poet capitulated by sending, without comment, the title poem, "The Black Riders," a haunting image of demon horsemen, personifications of sins, bursting terrifically out of the sea, brandishing swords and shields. Frederic Gordon, one of his studio friends who created the cover design, chose the orchid for a floral motif because he thought that this flower, "with its strange habits, extraordinary forms and curious properties,"[72] appropriately symbolized the radical structure and themes of the poems, characteristics Crane's mentor Howells did not admire. "These things," Howells wrote, returning copies Crane had sent him, "are too orphic for me. It is a pity for you to do them, for you can do things solid and real, so superbly."[73]

When Crane returned to the city in October, he took a small room near the Art Students' League building and set about looking for a reporter's job to supplement his meager income from his *Press* articles. One cold rainy day he appeared at Gordon's studio wet and coughing and racked with chills. He had been to see Edward Marshall about a job at the *World*, and Marshall had turned him down because he thought regular newspaper work would compromise him as an artist. Having no money for carfare and too proud to borrow from Marshall, he had walked all the way to the League building in a driving rain. Gordon had an extra bed and Crane, ill, stayed a week. When he recovered, he moved in with Gordon to continue work on *George's Mother*.

For his *Press* articles he drew often on narrative and descriptive bits and pieces in earlier writings. His picture in "Sailing Day Scene" of a chaotic crowd at a pier bidding emotional farewell to voyaging friends is cast largely in phrases and images adapted from descriptions of hotel crowds and harried baggagemen in Townley's *Tribune* column. A pompous ship's officer who strides before the agitated mob, "obviously vain in his clothes," is clearly an adaptation of the strutting and posturing officers of

The Red Badge.[74] "Mr. Binks' Day Off," a story turning on the contrast between the "warring metropolis" and the tranquil countryside, calls upon the novel and the Sullivan County sketches for its descriptions of numinous landscapes. Mr. Binks, a big city bank clerk, perceives in country vistas "the song of the universal religion, the mighty and mystic hymn of nature, whose melody is in each landscape,"[75] clearly versions of the pastoral scene which Henry Fleming's disordered imagination invests with monsters and demons.

In "Coney Island's Failing Days" a thoughtful observer of life on the beach, the stranger with "the tangled, philosophical hair," reflects on the profound incompatibility of human and natural orders. "[T]he sea always makes me feel that I am a trivial object," he says, and speculates on the relativity of all human values and the "unconscious calm insolence" of man's conventions in comparison with the laws of the "inexorable universe."[76] Ever wary of philosophical abstractions, Crane checks these profundities with sly irony, even though the ideas, as their constant implication in the themes of his fiction shows, are very much like his own. He also wrote two stories about studio life, whimsical sketches describing the egotistical humors of artists and illustrators and their struggles against dire poverty.[77] The characters, Great Grief, Corwinson, Little Pennoyer, and Purple Sanderson, are more or less caricatures of his studio friends, perhaps his revenge against those "Indians" for deriding his poems. Late in the year the *Press* printed several valuable sketches of New York street life, among them "The Fire," a tour de force description which evokes sinister intimations of demonism in the savage, irresistible flames of a burning building.[78] "When A Man Falls, A Crowd Gathers" is a penetrating study of crowd behavior in a minor crisis.[79]

Convinced that McClure, despite promises, was not going to publish *The Red Badge*, Crane called one day and took it away. It was a disappointing time. "As a matter of fact," he wrote Garland, "I have just crawled out of the fifty-third ditch into which I have been cast and now I feel I can write you a letter that wont make you ill. McClure was a Beast about the war-novel and that has been the thing that put me in one of the ditches. He kept it for six months until I was near mad. Oh, yes, he was going to use it, but—"[80] Crane took the manuscript, worn and dirty by now, to Irving Bacheller, proprietor of a struggling young newspaper syndicate, who remembered him that day as a thin, dark, "frail boy of unusual modesty." He

In the dark hall-way of the tenement three woman were quarreling animatedly and Their gestures made enormous shadows that, further back, mingled in terrific combat. A young girl came back from the street and brushed past them on her way up-stairs. They wheeled then instantly to watch her and ceased quarreling temporarily that they might criticise her

told Bacheller he "didn't know whether it was good or not" but "he needed money" and "had had enough of praise."[81] That night Bacheller and his wife took turns reading it aloud, and the next morning he sent for Crane and bought it for ninety dollars. His plan was to distribute it to his syndicate newspapers in January in a severely cut version which reduced it to about one-third of its full length. It was not what Crane had hoped for, but it was better than nothing—and he indisputably needed the money.

In mid-November he finished *George's Mother*. "I have just completed a New York book," he wrote Garland, "that leaves Maggie at the post. It is my best thing. Since you are not here, I am going to see if Mr. Howells will not read it."[82] Only a few days before, he had interviewed Howells for the *Press*, and when the critic, condemning sentimental novels of courtship, stressed the importance of writers who treat other subjects, such as "the relation of mother and son, of husband and wife, in fact all of these things that we live in continually," Crane slyly alluded to the story of a mother and her worthless son he was just then finishing. "I suppose there must be two or three new literary people just back of the horizon somewheres," Crane remarked. "[But] books upon these lines that you speak of are what might be called unpopular. Do you think them to be a profitable investment?"[83] It was a question born of his mood in those dark days.

Although historians have often assumed that Crane drew on such naturalistic novels as Zola's *L'Assommoir* for *George's Mother*, the principal source of his new novel was once again, as it had been with *Maggie* and *The Red Badge*, popular literature—this time the writings of the anti-saloon movement. Such melodramatic fictions as Timothy Shay Arthur's *Ten Nights in a Barroom* (1854) and its sequel, *Three Years in a Mantrap* (1872) had made the staple elements of the drunkard's story familiar to everyone: the blighting of the drunkard's career, the impoverishment of the victim's family, and the death of a loved one—child, wife, or mother—from abuse or neglect. These stereotypical elements Crane adapted to personal history, modeling George's rebellion against the sentimental piety of Mrs. Kelcey on his own rejections of Mrs. Crane's "vacuous, futile, psalm-singing" religiosity in the mid-eighties and drawing on the heroes of his earlier fiction for George's swaggering egotism and vulnerability to illusion. The plot he contrived from these unexceptional materials, transmuted by the distancing effect of his irony and the pictorial brilliance of his descriptions, owed much of its satirical power to his skeptical feelings toward Methodist piety and the sentimental heroics of popular literature of the day.

Though the Kelceys live in the same tenement the Johnsons occupy, they are very different. Mrs. Kelcey is a scrupulous homemaker and fastidious moralist. She dotes on the self-centered George, whose chief concern is the hateful indifference of the world to his superior virtues. He finds proper appreciation, however, in the corner saloon, where he falls in with a crowd of loafers headed by old Bleecker, whose suave amiability and infinite knowledge of cocktails George deeply admires. Alcohol and the flattery of Bleecker and his friends feed his growing resentment of his mother's sentimental moralizing. He becomes callous and abusive. He loses his job, and when he is abandoned by his saloon friends, who suddenly turn cold and unsympathetic when he tries to borrow money, he drifts into a gang of street toughs. His mother's conviction that George is a brilliant, clever son, destined for greatness, is eventually dispelled. She falls ill and seems to lose the will to live. When George receives word that she is dying of a stroke, he is about to fight a member of his gang, Blue Billy, to settle a dispute over shares in a bucket of stolen beer.

What makes this plot interesting, of course, is once again wholly a matter of Crane's treatment of it. The preposterous vulgarity of the saloon crowd, the mindless banality of their talk, their tawdry sentimentality, comical swagger, and self-congratulatory complacency are admirably portrayed. In their retreat to the back room of the saloon from "a grinding world filled with men who were harsh," these comrades "understood that they were true and tender spirits," that they possessed "various virtues which were unappreciated by those with whom they were commonly obliged to mingle." The style is often broadly parodic, as in the scene where two of these congenial spirits are suddenly and forcibly struck by the extraordinary depth of their mutual admiration:

> Once old Bleecker stared at Jones for a few moments. Suddenly he broke out: "Jones, you're one of the finest fellows I ever knew!" A flush of pleasure went over the other's face, and then he made a modest gesture, the protest of an humble man. "Don't flimflam me, ol' boy," he said, with earnestness. But Bleecker roared that he was serious about it. The two men arose and shook hands emotionally. Jones bunted against the table and knocked off a glass.

Afterward a general hand-shaking was inaugurated. Brotherly sentiments flew about the room. There was an uproar of fraternal feeling.[84]

The issue of fraternal feeling, the possibility of human brotherhood, is constant in Crane's work from the Sullivan County sketches through the Whilomville tales. The obvious skepticism in this satirical treatment of the theme can perhaps be traced to the maudlin "love feasts" of the Methodist camp or to the emotional handshaking "in token of brotherly love" the Reverend Yatman inspired at an Ocean Grove revival Crane reported to the *Tribune* in 1888. The theme is treated more sympathetically, though still critically, in *The Red Badge* and "The Open Boat," but in the Sullivan County sketches and *George's Mother*, the comradeship of men is more problematical and uncertain, threatened by expansive emotions of the self. The description of Bleecker's party, which satirizes the stereotyped tastes, crippled thought, and vulgar emotions of the guests, of whom George is typical, is especially memorable. Mr. Zuesentell's nervous recitation of "Patrick Clancy's Pig," the comical social helplessness of some of the timid guests, the pompous self-confidence of Bleecker, and the ultimate dissolution of the party in a blur of absurd alcoholic violence are vividly rendered in Crane's best impressionistic style.

Howells read the novel in manuscript, but what he or Crane did to find a publisher for it is not known. It presumably made the round of editors, but if so, it was soon laid aside while Crane pursued other matters. He had arranged with Bacheller for an assignment to the Far West as a roving correspondent. Crane, who anticipated journeys compulsively all his life, began preparing for an immediate departure. But the trip was delayed, perhaps because Bacheller had decided to distribute the truncated war novel to his syndicate in December rather than in January, as originally planned, and wanted Crane in New York. In any case, on December 3 the first installment of the sadly mutilated novel appeared in the *Philadelphia Press* and a week later in the *New York Press*.

The newspaper world was impressed by *The Red Badge*, and Crane was surprised to discover shortly that he had become a minor local celebrity. An editorial in the *Philadelphia Press* predicted future fame for him, and his friend E. J. Edwards, a journalist who had seen a preliminary, partial draft of the novel in the spring of 1893, wrote a piece for the *Press* in which he noted that the author's special distinction was his "great power, of real imagination, and a sort of poetic quality" which took him "out of the list of the perfunctory realists." Edwards, who wrote under the name "Holland," was convinced that Crane was destined to become "the most powerful of American tellers of tales."[85] Talcott Williams of the *Philadelphia Press* asked Bacheller to bring the author to Philadelphia. When Crane appeared in the press room, editors, reporters, proofreaders, and compositors crowded around to offer congratulations. From the Continental Hotel he wrote Linson that Bacheller had asked for the loan of the portrait the artist had painted of him a few months earlier. Bacheller, sure that this was the beginning of Crane's fame, was apparently anticipating demands for his likeness.

When he returned to New York, he stopped briefly at the League building to answer letters from Copeland and Day, and then departed for Port Jervis, ready to start his trip on a moment's notice. But the journey was delayed again, and he was soon back in the city, where he discovered that New York editors had become much interested in him. Ripley Hitchcock, of Appleton and Company, asked for samples of his work, and Crane gave him clippings of a few of his *Press* sketches. When Hitchcock asked if he had something longer, he doubtfully mentioned *The Red Badge*, which "some of the boys in the office seemed to like," and shortly sent the editor clippings of the newspaper version—"much smaller and to my mind much worse than its original form."[86] In early January 1895, responding to Copeland and Day's request for items to use in advertising *The Black Riders*, he sent a copy of "Holland's" comments on the novel and mentioned Garland's *Arena* review of *Maggie*. "I have a good many notices," he wrote, "but none of them are particular. Most of them call me a prominent youth." He wanted to dedicate *The Black Riders* to Garland, he advised the publishers, "in just one line, no more: To Hamlin Garland."[87]

Toward the end of January, after so many delays and changes in plans, he was launched at last on his Western journey. He had not heard anything before he left about *The Red Badge*, which Hitchcock had by now seen in the full manuscript version, and Crane wrote for news from St. Louis, adding a word to buttress whatever good opinion Hitchcock might have of the novel. "If you had not read the story, I would wish you to hear the *Philadelphia Press* staff speak of it. When I was there some days ago, I was amazed to hear the way in which they talked of it."[88] In

Another photo used by Linson in his study for Crane's portrait, 1894 (courtesy Syracuse University)

For the benefit of his friends by

Caricature of Crane by Linson on the occasion of his departure to the West in January 1895 (courtesy Barrett Collection, University of Virginia)

Corwin Knapp Linson's portrait of Crane, 1894 (courtesy Barrett
Collection, University of Virginia)

mid-February, in Lincoln, Nebraska, he got word from Hitchcock that Appleton and Company had accepted his book for publication, a turn in fortune that probably saved the novel from destruction. Crane told someone later that he had decided to burn it if Appleton rejected it.

If he was elated by this news, he kept his feelings to himself. To Willa Cather, an admiring young *Nebraska State Journal* reporter and aspiring novelist who had corrected proof for *The Red Badge* when the *Journal* printed it in early December, Crane seemed depressed and bitter. If he had known that the four innovative books he had written in the iron effort of his two-and-a-half-year sojourn in poverty would one day be identified as important markers in the history of American writing, and that the book now about to come before the public would in time be acknowledged as an American classic, he might have found greater satisfaction in Hitchcock's news. As it was, his answer to the editor was notably subdued: "I've just recieved your letter. I would be glad to have Appleton and Co publish the story on those terms. I am going from here to New Orleans. The Mss could be corrected by me there in short order."[89] And then he turned his attention to the state of affairs in the Far West.

FOUR

THE WEST, MEXICO, AND NEW YORK

CRANE had originally thought to make Nevada his first destination on the Western tour, but in late December stories in Eastern newspapers about a disastrous drought in Nebraska brought about a change in plans. Nelly Bly's articles in the *New York World* describing the sufferings in the stricken state had aroused much interest, and Bacheller decided to send Crane there for a first-hand report for the Bacheller-Johnson Syndicate. Arriving in Lincoln from St. Louis in the early evening of February 1, 1895, he went at once to the offices of the *Nebraska State Journal,* where he met the managing editor and a young part-time reporter named Willa Cather. Ambitious to be a writer herself, Cather studied Crane closely. She had copyedited *The Red Badge of Courage* in December for the *Journal,* a Bacheller Syndicate subscriber, and having seen "the wonder of that re-markable performance," was surprised to find its author, the first real writer she had ever seen, so unimpressive. "He was thin to emaciation, his face was gaunt and unshaven, a thin dark moustache straggled on his upper lip, his black hair grew low on his forehead and was shaggy and unkempt. His grey clothes were much the worse for wear and fitted him so badly it seemed unlikely he had ever been measured for them." She remembered particularly his striking eyes, "large and dark and full of lustre and changing lights, but with a profound melancholy always lurking deep in them."[1]

He was in and out of the office, depressed and uncommunicative. Cather, trying to draw him out on literature, once asked him what he thought of Maupassant, a writer she particularly admired, and he replied sarcastically, "Oh, you're Moping, are you?" and went on reading a volume of Poe he had brought with him. After a few days he left for Eddyville, 125 miles west in Dawson County in the heart of the drought country. He was probably in Kearney, forty miles short of his destination, when a ferocious blizzard struck, bringing winds of more than sixty miles per hour and dropping temperatures to eighteen degrees below zero. He reached Eddyville somehow and found the town paralyzed from the blast of the bitter wind. Like Fort Romper in the blizzard in "The Blue Hotel," the town was deserted, a mere straggle of dim and silent houses huddling in the terrible fury of the storm. In the remote countryside he saw horses standing "abjectly and stolidly in the fields, their backs humped and turned toward the eye of the wind, their heads near the ground, their manes blowing over their eyes," their soft noses crusted with ice. He interviewed a farmer who said he got no help from the government relief program, and Crane asked him how he got along. "Don't git along, stranger. Who the hell told you I did get along?"[2]

Back in Lincoln he routinely interviewed the governor and the state relief director, and then in a somber mood, waiting for money from Bacheller which was late coming, he wrote a masterly sketch, "Nebraska's Bitter Fight for Life." He had heard about the killing heat during the drought the summer before, and juxtaposing images from these stories against vivid pictures of the blizzard he had just experienced, he created a memorable vision of the awesome depredations of nature. He described the summer agony of a land scorched by a "terrible and inscrutable wrath of nature," a screaming wind, "hot as an oven's fury," that raged over the rich brown crops "like a pestilence" while the farmers stood by in helpless despair. "It was as if upon the massive altar of the earth, their homes and their families were being offered in sacrifice to the wrath of some blind and pitiless deity." The blizzard, a "strange and unspeakable punishment of nature," brought winds from the north that swept over the devastated countryside like "wolves of ice." The graphic imagery of tempest-driven snowflakes "fleeing into the south, traversing as level as a line of bullets, speeding like the wind,"[3] he used nearly three years later in "The Blue Hotel": "great whirls and clouds of flakes, swept up from the ground by the frantic winds, were streaming southward with the speed of bullets."[4]

The night before he left Lincoln for New Orleans, via Kansas City and Hot Springs, he came into the *Journal* office late, just as Cather was finishing a review of a play. He sat by the open window and talked to her for the first time about his life as a writer. He said he could not live by writing fiction because it took too long to bring the cluttering detail of his experience into meaningful order. "The detail of a thing has to filter through my blood, and then it comes out like a native product, but it takes forever."[5]

His dispatch from Hot Springs, Arkansas, describes the town in well-tried images of resort life—lively crowds and harried baggagemen; but he also touched briefly on another ready-made theme, the modernity of the West—adapted, like many of his ideas, from popular culture. The rapid encroachment of Eastern civilization on the old Wild West was a familiar subject in popular writings of the day, and Crane himself had written about it in "A Christmas Dinner Won in Battle," a story which had appeared in the *Plumber's Trade Journal* in December.[6] In this trifle he had described how the raw plains town of Levelville had become a "dignified city" by acquiring modern plumbing, a board of aldermen, policemen in uniform (to the discomfort of cowboys who come in for their regular Saturday night celebrations), and blueprint plans for a street railway three miles long, the germ of the theme which informs his classic Western, "The Bride Comes to Yellow Sky."

In New Orleans a few days later he was in high spirits, writing Linson a whimsical letter in mock French and German: "Friedweller die schonën-berger je suis dans New Orleans. Cracked ice dans Nebraska, terra del fuego dans New Orleans."[7] He found the city engaging and stimulating. As his dispatch "The Fete of Mardi Gras" shows, the gay mummery of the procession, the surge and sway of the great crowds, and the noisy confusion and high color, which "had all the distinctness of a marvellous painting," fired his imagination.[8] He received the typescript of *The Red Badge* from Hitchcock and returned it early in March "arranged" for the printer. "I made a great number of small corrections," he wrote from Galveston, chiefly additions and deletions of words and phrases. But he also added the sentimental last sentence, "Over the river a golden ray of sun came through the hosts of leaden rain clouds," a final ironic mockery of Henry's complacent sense of security in what he takes to be the special regard of a benign nature. Hitchcock had asked Crane while he was still in Lincoln to suggest a shorter title, and the author had asked for time to think it over. When he returned the corrected typescript, he wrote, "As to the name I am unable to see what to do with it unless the word "Red" is cut out, perhaps. That would shorten it."[9]

He found Galveston and San Antonio proof that the old West existed largely in the romantic visions of overly expectant visitors. Travelers anxious to confirm heroic legends "grab tradition in wonder," he wrote, and it is this that "has kept the sweeping march of the West," with its paved streets, webs of telegraph wires, and clamorous trolleys, "from being chronicled in any particularly true fashion."[10] From San Antonio he protested against "an eloquent description of the town which makes it consist of three old ruins and a row of Mexicans sitting in the sun" when it is actually "a totally modern" city with "rows of handsome business blocks" and "the terrible and almighty trolly car." His preoccupation with the theme reveals a yearning for the legendary which his skepticism was constantly called on to suppress. The legend of the Alamo, "the greatest memorial to courage which civilization has allowed to stand," appealed to his sense of the heroic; but a passage that celebrates the "inverted courage" of a man who deserted shows how vulnerable his idea of the heroic was to the constant wash of his irony. When the commander, Colonel Travis, called his men together to tell them their fate was sealed, that all must die, one Rose, "some kind of a dogged philosopher," refused the role of sacrificial hero. "There is," Crane wrote, "a strange inverted courage in the manner in which he faced his companions with this sudden and short refusal in the midst of a general exhibition of supreme bravery. 'No,' he said. He bade them adieu and climbed the wall. Upon its top he turned to look down at the upturned faces of his silent comrades."[11] The suspended moments seems to concentrate for Crane the whole ambivalent question of the heroic.

He rescued a derelict boy he found sobbing in Alamo Plaza—sixteen-year-old Edward Grover. The youth had come west from Chicago to be a cowboy, but his money had run out, and he was now stranded penniless in

San Antonio. Crane bought him a ticket home, and later wrote him a bantering note of advice from "a tough jay from back East"—"stay home and grow a mustache before you rush out into the red universe any more."[12] He wrote Dr. Lucius Button, formerly of the Pendennis Club, to joke him about his hometown of Akron, Ohio, describing "a most intolerable duffer" he met in New Orleans, an "ingenuous Akron spirit" whose countrified amazement at everything he saw was acutely embarrassing. "He had fingers like lightning rods and on the street he continually pointed at various citizens with the exclamation: 'Look at that fellow!' People in New Orleans don't like that sort of thing, you know. I'm off for Mexico tonight."[13]

In his fine account of the train ride to Mexico City, he whimsically cast himself and Charles Gardner, a Chicago engineer he met in San Antonio, in fictional roles, Gardner being the "capitalist from Chicago" and Crane the "archaeologist from Boston." As their train entered the mesquite country of northern Mexico, the expectations of the travellers, "hungry for color, form, action," rose and rose. The spectacle of Mexican life registered powerfully on his imagination. In the mysterious landscape and impassive mien of the people he found intimations of some alien and elusive meaning. He was impressed by "the inscrutable visage" of a sheepherder, by "the masses of crimson rays" from household fires in a village at dusk where "dark and sinister shadows moved," by the empty, blazing skies of Mexican noons, by mountains that "stand like gods on the world" and silence the speech of men who "fear that they might hear." The stark, rugged landscape and primitive life of the people, the very air itself, seemed to accentuate primary attributes of nature. "[T]he atmosphere seldom softens anything. It devotes its energy to making high lights, bringing everything forward, making colors fairly volcanic."[14]

But intimations of menace, he discovered, were not always literary or metaphysical. In April, on an excursion into the Mexican back country, Crane and his guide, Miguel Itorbide, were asleep in a primitive village inn when they were awakened by the arrival of a troop of horsemen led by the bandit Ramón Colorado. Crane heard Colorado talking in the next room about robbing him, but the bandit was distracted by the arrival of several women. At dawn Crane and his guide slipped off, mounted their horses, and raced into the desert. The bandits gave chase and were gaining steadily on them when a company of mounted police appeared and drove them away. Crane later based a story on the incident: "One Dash—Horses," a vivid evocation of a feeling of crisis, furious motion, and touching rapport between horse and rider. The hero is the swift little pony, which responds in a desperate moment with admirable devotion and determination.[15]

He was in Puebla in late April, his face tanned "the color of a brick sidewalk" and with nothing American about him "save a large Smith and Wesson revolver," when he saw an American girl in a party of tourists and was reminded of Nellie Crouse,[16] a young woman he had met briefly at a tea in New York shortly before his departure in January. He was suddenly homesick. He was in New York by mid-May, tired and unwell but cheered by the publication of *The Black Riders*, which had come out only a few days before he arrived. Irving Bacheller initiated him into his newly-formed Lanthorne Club, a group of journalists and writers whose head-quarters was a quaint old roof house over a stable yard in William Street, where they entertained at luncheons famous guests like Howells, Mark Twain, and Rudyard Kipling. The "Lanterns," as they called themselves, were ardent poker players, and Crane, who shared their passion for the game, promptly lost a handful of opals he had brought from Mexico. One of the Lanterns, Willis Brooks Hawkins, poker player and editor of the Brains Publishing Company, "a man of playful whims and quaint and delightful fancies," became one of the few intimate friends he ever had.

In late May or early June, he was at Ed's House in Hartwood, writing Copeland and Day for news about the sale of *The Black Riders*. "I see they are making some stir," he said,[17] referring probably to Harry Thurston Peck's review in the May *Bookman*. Peck said Crane was "the Aubrey Beardsley of poetry," whose odd, unrhymed, unmetrical verses, printed entirely in capitals and bound in bizarre black and white covers, were proof that he was "bidding for renown wholly on the basis of his eccentricity." But like Beardsley, "with all his absurdities," the critic added a bit inconsistently, Crane was "a true poet whose verse, long after the eccentricity of its form has worn off, fascinates us and forbids us to lay the volume down until the last line has been read."[18] A scorching review in the *Tribune* identified him as one of the outrageous "New Poets" whose verses, in "their futility and affectation," appear to "the impartial reader as so much trash."[19] Their radical form puzzled many readers, including Howells, who reviewed them coolly in *Harper's* some months later; but a few, like Peck and T. W. Higginson, acknowledged that Crane's apparent affectations were "not really such." His real distinction, Higginson wrote, was "a vigorous earnestness and a fresh pair of eyes."[20]

He was in and out of the city in June and July, working for Bacheller. He sent the editor "A Mystery of Heroism," a workmanlike Civil War story about a soldier who charges across a field under heavy fire to fetch a bucket of water from a distant well, as well as two or three articles on Mexico; but he was mostly marking time, anticipating the publication of *The Red Badge* and keeping up with reviews of *The Black Riders*. In early September he was in Philadelphia looking for a job with the *Press*, and for a moment it looked as if he had one. "It is dramatic criticism and nuthin else," he wrote Hawkins jubilantly. "I've taken it and am to go to work at once." But a few days later he wrote again. "Things fell ker-plunk. Stranded here in Phila." He stayed on a while with friends and began "One Dash—Horses," writing Hawkins that he was working on a story about his "personal troubles in Mexico."[21] He was soon back in New York, camping for a few days at a boarding house on West 23rd Street, and then after a big farewell poker party with Hawkins and other friends, he retreated again to Hartwood and Port Jervis.

After the arduous western journey and years of rigorous city life, the serene atmosphere of these rural villages was a welcome respite. He played cops and robbers with his nieces and donned white flannel trousers for croquet and tennis with young men and women vacationing at the resort hotels. A superb horseman, he spent hours riding the hill trails. Sometimes he sailed a boat on the lake or hunted in the woody hills. In the mornings he sat on Will's front porch in a large wicker chair, screened by a syringa bush, and wrote, sending the disappointed children away when they hunted him out there. When *The Red Badge* was published in October, he had already started another novel for Appleton, tentatively called "The Eternal Patience," later titled *The Third Violet*; but his chatty letters to Willis Hawkins about life in Hartwood say little about either book. He seemed more interested in the fall woods, horses, and partridges than in the fate of *The Red Badge*. At the end of October he wrote Hitchcock that he had roughed out seven chapters of a new novel, a story about a summer romance between a young painter home from his New York studio and a charming heiress vacationing at a local resort. These drafted chapters, he assured Hitchcock wryly, had given him "the proper enormous interest in the theme."[22]

Title page of The Red Badge of Courage, *1895* (courtesy Barrett Collection, University of Virginia)

The Red Badge Of Courage

An Episode of the American Civil War

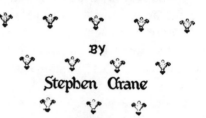

BY

Stephen Crane

New York
D· Appleton and Company
1895

THE BLACK RIDERS AND
OTHER LINES BY STE–
PHEN CRANE

BOSTON COPELAND AND DAY MDCCCXCV

Title page of The Black Riders, *1895* (courtesy Barrett Collection, University of Virginia)

Crane in early 1896, when he was becoming famous as the author of
The Red Badge of Courage *(courtesy Lilly Library, Indiana*
University)

Nellie Crouse, who inspired Crane's sudden return from Mexico in 1895 (courtesy Syracuse University)

Crane in Washington, D.C., 1895 (courtesy Barrett
Collection, University of Virginia)

If Howells's unenthusiastic review of *The Red Badge* in *Harper's Weekly* in late October disappointed Crane, he did not mention it. Other war writers, Howells observed, had given a more realistic sense of battle, and though the book on the "psychological side" was "worthwhile," its greater significance was in its promise of better things to come "from a new talent working upon a high level, not quite clearly as yet, but strenuously."[23] He was as kind as he could be, given his critical prejudices; for actually, as he made clear later, he thought the war novel a mistake, a regrettable diversion, as *The Black Riders* had been, from serious literary purposes.

But by mid-November, as the Port Jervis *Union* reported, *The Red Badge* had been lauded by reviewers from Boston to Minneapolis for its dramatic intensity and vivid imagery, qualities many reviewers, unlike Howells, took as proof of its unsurpassed realism. Crane wrote Hawkins that a clipping bureau in Boston had sent him forty-one reviews. "And, oh, say, most of 'em were not only favorable but passionately enthusiastic," he exulted. "They didn't skirmish around and say maybe—perhaps—if—after a time—it is possible—under certain circumstances—but. No; they were cocksure," though about six, he said, were unfavorable, and the "grind" in the *Tribune* was the worst. He apologized for dwelling so long on his growing fame. "It sounds sort of priggish, somehow. And it is I have no doubt excepting that it is right to be elated when almost all the writers and reviewers seem to have really read the thing."[24] He was suddenly in demand. Appleton decided to publish the new novel in its new Zeit-Geist Series; and McClure, who had no doubt pondered long his missed opportunity with the novel, engaged him to write more war stories. About mid-month he reluctantly began "The Little Regiment." "It is awfully hard," he wrote Hawkins. "I have invented the sum of my invention in regard to war and this story keeps me in internal despair."[25]

In December, the Society of Philistines of East Aurora, New York, headed by the tireless publicity-seeker Elbert Hubbard, honored Crane with a formal testimonial dinner. The chief purpose of the Society was to contend against the Eastern literary establishment, often satirically characterized as hopelessly dull and unprogressive in the Society's irreverent little magazine, the *Philistine*. The magazine had printed several of Crane's poems, and when *The Black Riders* brought him notoriety as a radical young poet, the Society conceived the dinner—to which with much fanfare it invited scores of writers, journalists, and editors—as a convenient means of advancing its cause. Held at the Genesee House in Buffalo on December 19, the dinner turned out to be a raucous affair with much noisy joking and bantering interruption of the speakers—a deplorable exhibition of bad taste, according to some of the guests, who thought Crane had been ill used by the publicity-conscious Hubbard. The *Lotus*, the *Philistine*'s arch rival, reported sarcastically that the guest of honor was made "the butt of the sparkling wit of some of our best litterateurs."[26] But Crane's speech, according to the *Bookman*, "scintillated with flashes of wit, to the merriment of all,"[27] and he seemed to enjoy the occasion, aware though he must have been of Hubbard's motives.

A few days after this affair Crane mailed the manuscript of *The Third Violet* to Hitchcock. Only a little over two months in the writing, it had been quick, easy work, and he had never had much confidence in it. "I am not sure that it is any good," he had written Hawkins when it was about one-third finished; and when it was half done, "It seems clever sometimes and sometimes it seems nonsensical."[28] When he mailed the novel to Appleton, he wrote, "I've an idea it won't be accepted. It's pretty rotten work. I used myself up in the accursed "Red Badge.' "[29]

It may be that he was trying in *The Third Violet* to take Howells's hint that his talent would be better used for social realism than for impressionistic and "orphic" writings like *The Red Badge* and *The Black Riders*. But Howellsian realism was beyond his grasp. He had little gift for sustained specification of realistic detail and none of the true realist's mastery of the intricacies of social codes and conventions. Except in his description of the nearly wordless courtship in "The Pace of Youth," he never wrote successfully about romantic love, and *The Third Violet* is arguably the most inconsequential of his books. For the plot he attempted to weave together two strands of autobiography: his love affairs with Helen Trent and Lily Munroe and his experiences among artists and illustrators in the Art Students' League building, which he had used already in his 1894 "Stories Told by an Artist." The courtship begins when Billie Hawker meets Miss Grace Fanhall at a summer vacation hotel and continues after the couple returns to the city, Hawker to his ramshackle studio and Miss Fanhall to her elegant town house. The story ends when Hawker, after much confusion caused by Miss Fanhall's ladylike coyness (which Crane obviously admires as a sign of her true womanhood), finally understands that the lady "cares for him," a point she makes esoterically by giving her lover, on three different occasions, a gift of a single violet. There is a fine portrait of Hawker's awkward and endearing Irish setter, Stanley, a character drawn from Will's much-adored dog Chester, and some lively description of studio life; but aside from these happy touches the writing could hardly be identified as Crane's. He knew himself that it was alien to his vision and method, and when Hitchcock suggested rewriting it to give it more substance, he declined: "I think it is as well to go ahead with The Third Violet. People may just as well discover now that the high dramatic key of The Red Badge cannot be sustained. . . . I dont think The Red Badge to be any great shakes but then the very theme of it gives it an intensity that a writer cant reach every day."[30]

One of the many ironies of Crane's life is that just as he finished one of his worst books he became internationally famous. Within a month after the London publisher Heinemann brought out *The Red Badge* at the end of November, it was among the most popular books in England. Joseph Conrad wrote later that the sensation it produced was one of the enduring memories of his literary life; and H. G. Wells recalled the deep admiration of the English literary world for "its freshness of method, its vigor of imagination, its force of color and its essential freedom from many traditions that dominate this side of the Atlantic. . . ." It was widely acknowledged in England, he wrote, as "a new thing, in a new school."[31] Harold Frederic, American novelist and London correspondent for the *New York Times*, wrote a laudatory review which appeared in the *Times* at the end of January, and it was reviewed for months in English newspapers and literary magazines. Frederic's article and the English reviews stimulated new interest in the book in America, and between January and June, 1896, it was on best-seller lists in nearly every major city in the country.

The elation Crane felt over his success was short-lived. He discovered in trying to meet demands from editors for more war stories that he had little to say about the very subject that had made him famous. On a whim he had begun a correspondence with Nellie Crouse, the young Akron, Ohio, woman who, as he wrote her in December, had inspired his sudden departure from Mexico seven months before. To this beautiful young woman, whom he had seen only once and then only briefly at an afternoon tea in New York, he poured out his decidedly mixed feelings about fame, his pride on the one hand in his success and his anxiety on the other about his future as a writer, especially his future as a war writer. "I am engaged in rowing with people who wish me to write more war-stories," he wrote her. "Hang all war-stories."[32] He began to derogate *The Red Badge*, referring to it slightingly on various occasions as the "damned 'Red Badge,'" "That damned book," "the accursed 'Red Badge.'" He wrote Crouse that he had once thought it "a pretty good thing," but that he now no longer cared much for it.[33] He warned McClure that their arrangement for more war stories might not be to the publisher's advantage. "I am perfectly satisfied with my end of it," he said, "but your end somewhat worries me for I am often inexpressibly dull and uncreative and these periods often last for days"; and again, "I feel for you when I think of some of the things of mine which you will have to read or have read."[34] Though he rarely mentioned *The Third Violet* after he sent it to Hitchcock, his sense of it as a failure would not have encouraged him to continue this kind of writing, either. Fame, as it seemed, was putting him to a severe test.

By the end of January he had discovered another disadvantage in fame, a certain danger in the adulation of the literary world. Visiting the city to see editors and friends, he found himself besieged by admirers, and he rushed back to Hartwood in a kind of panic without keeping his appointments. "I couldn't breathe in that accursed tumult," he wrote Hawkins. "On Friday it had me keyed to a point where I was no more than a wild beast and I had to make a dash willy-nilly."[35] To Hitchcock, he wrote in a note of apology: "I had grown used to being called a damned ass but this sudden new admiration of my friends has made a gibbering idiot of me. I shall stick to my hills."[36] He wrote Howells that one advantage of these hills was that he could "shout triumphant shouts" if he pleased without being heard. "However I have not elected to shout any shouts. I am, mostly afraid. Afraid that some small degree of talk will turn me ever so slightly from what I believe to be the pursuit of truth, and that my block-head will lose something of the resolution which carried me very comfortably through the ridicule."[37] He wrote Nellie Crouse that he felt compelled to face the challenge of his fame with "desperate resolution." Reading the English reviews and laudatory letters about *The Black Riders*, he said he saw for the first time "the majestic forces which are arrayed against man's true success—not the world—the world is silly, changeable, any of it's decisions can be reversed—but man's own colossal impulses more strong than chains, and I perceived that the fight was not going to be with the world but with yourself."[38]

Fame forced him to reflect anew on his purposes and convictions, and he reaffirmed, in one of his most revealing statements of his aesthetic, his independence of binding conventions of art and life. "I understand," he wrote an editor, "that a man is born into the world with his own pair of eyes, and he is not at all responsible for his vision—he is merely responsible for his quality of personal honesty. To keep close to this personal honesty is my supreme ambition. There is a sublime egotism in talking of honesty. I, however, do not say that I am honest. I merely say that I am as nearly honest as a weak mental machinery will allow. This aim in life struck me as being the only thing worth while. A man is sure to fail at it, but there is something in the failure."[39] In its recognition of the powers of a narrowing vanity to distort and of the maddening elusiveness of reality, this puts on the artist no responsibility for ultimate truths, but merely the responsibility to represent faithfully what he sees, or thinks he sees. Ford Madox Ford and Joseph Conrad adapted the view to the aesthetics of fiction they would one day work out in collaboration, inspired partly by the examples of *The Red Badge* and "The Open Boat."

But the war stories he was writing for McClure had little to do with these aims, as Crane must have known. He had finished five by the end of February: "The Little Regiment," "The Veteran," "Three Miraculous Soldiers," "An Indiana Campaign," and "An Episode of War." He sent the first three, and perhaps others, to McClure, but only two, "The Veteran" and "The Little Regiment," appeared in *McClure's Magazine*. He described "The Little Regiment" to the editor of the *Critic* as "a novelette . . . which represents my work at its best I think," but he knew it reflected, like the others, his distressing uncertainty as a war writer. "[It] is positively my last thing dealing with battle," he added.[40]

The tendency in the stories, which Appleton published in book form in late 1896 as *The Little Regiment*, is toward a more conventional realism. Crane drew heavily on *The Red Badge* for metaphors and images, but he used them more to describe perceptions of the narrator than to represent illusions and anxieties of the characters. The fanciful visions of the alienated Henry, whose distressed psychological life provides a colorful and dramatic version of reality in the novel, appear in the stories fitfully and incidentally. The radical conflict between man and nature that accounts for much of the intensity and symbolic resonance of *The Red Badge* is largely absent. The heroes of the stories are more or less realistic social types, more normally rational and judgmental than Henry and his prototypes. In "A Mystery of Heroism," Fred Collins, unlike Henry, is reflective and critical, conscious of his vanity and of its ethical and social significance. The menace in the shell-blasted field is Confederate artillery, not a specter-demon born of Collins's guilt or terror. "An Indiana Campaign" gently satirizes old Major Tom Boldin and the folks of Migglesville for their unsophisticated reaction to an idle rumor that a Rebel soldier is hiding in a neighboring cornfield. The young girl of "Three Miraculous Soldiers" has a tendency—like that of her very distant fictional cousin Henry—to imagine colorful heroics, but her sound common sense banishes these "gorgeous contrivances and expedients of fiction" as she plans the escape of three friendly soldiers imprisoned by the enemy in her father's barn. The title story, "The Little Regiment," is about two brothers whose strong mutual affection is concealed by their constant bickering. The function of the battles, profusely and somewhat pointlessly described, is merely to provide the incident that reveals their true feelings. Three months in the writing, this story involved Crane, as he said, in "a daily battle with a tangle of facts and emotions,"[41] a symptom of the crisis of confidence brought on by his growing reputation as a war writer.

More interesting by far is "The Veteran," a short sequel to *The Red Badge* which tells how Henry Fleming as an old man sacrifices his life trying to rescue two colts from a burning barn. It points clearly to an important development in Crane's style. The lean, disciplined prose moves the story rapidly from Henry's account of his flight from his first battle to the sharp description of his final rush into the blazing barn, just before the roof falls in. It is not a war story, strictly, though it draws on the war imagery of the novel. The story begins with a glimpse of "a meadow . . . resplendent in spring-time green," a fleeting vision of that spring long ago when young Henry found the idyllic landscape suddenly filled with "red and green dragons." Telling the story of his flight, old Henry can now appreciate "some comedy in this recital." The enemy, he remembers, appeared as "a lot of flitting figures," and he recalls thinking at the moment of panic that "the sky was falling down," that "the world was coming to an end." But the terror now is not imaginary war demons but the real terror of a burning barn. When he hurls open the door, a yellow flame leaps out and speeds "frantically up the old grey wall. It [is] glad, terrible, this single flame, like the wild banner of deadly and triumphant foes." This image of satanic fire, "laden with tones of hate and death, a hymn of wonderful ferocity," crosses with the image of demonic war, and old Henry, rushing into the inferno, challenges at last the inscrutable wrath of nature he thought he had triumphed over at the end of his first battle long ago. The story skillfully adapts Crane's familiar symbols to a new style, the style essentially of "The Open Boat," a story "after the fact," as the subtitle says, but one which, like "The Veteran," is composed of elements drawn obliquely from his mythic imagination.

McClure proposed a series of articles on famous Civil War battles, but Crane was doubtful, and after a hurried visit to the battlefield at Fredericksburg, declined the project, finding little interest in the idea of becoming a war historian. He turned his attention to revising *Maggie*, which Appleton wanted to republish, and to arranging for the publication of *George's Mother*. He began reworking *Maggie* in February, smoothing out grammar and phrasing, deleting profanities, and canceling the graphic description at the end of chapter 17 of the "huge fat man in torn and greasy garments" Maggie meets on her way to the river. He gave *George's Mother* to the publisher Edward Arnold, violating, as he admitted not too apologetically to Hitchcock, "certain business courtesies," since Appleton presumably had first call on the book.

McClure also thought he might write a novel about politics and sent him to Washington about mid-March to study the scene, especially the behavior of congressmen; but by the end of the month Crane had given up the idea. "These men pose so hard," he wrote Hitchcock, "that it would take a double-barreled shotgun to disclose their inward feelings and I despair of knowing them."[42] Miss Crouse, meanwhile, had hinted her disapproval of his unconventional attitudes and habits, which he had discussed freely in his remarkable letters to her, and he wrote a mournful last note from Washington, assuming the role of the devastated rejected lover. "If there is a joy of living I cant find it. The future? The future is blue with obligations—new trials—conflicts. It was a rare old wine the *gods brewed* for mortals. Flagons of despair."[43]

By the beginning of April he was in New York, engaged once again as a free-lance journalist, contributing over the next several months more than twenty articles and stories to the Bacheller and McClure syndicates and the *New York Journal*. "A Tale of Mere Chance," a Poesque fantasy about a murderer relentlessly pursued by his guilty conscience, is the least characteristic of the stories. For the others he drew on familiar materials—city life, Texas and Mexico, the Civil War. "A Freight Car Incident," a tale about an irascible two-gun desperado who terrifies a prairie town, vaguely anticipates "The Bride Comes to Yellow Sky"; and three stories describe the Mexican adventures of a pair of insouciant pranksters known as the New York Kid and the San Francisco Kid. In August he wrote a piece for the *Journal* on Asbury Park, where he found the eccentric James A. Bradley, one of his favorite satirical targets in his early newspaper days, as vulnerable to his wit as ever. "[R]ed whiskers of the Icelandic lichen pattern grow fretfully upon his chin," he wrote, observing that the venerable Founder was still putting up moral signs on the beach to "improve the effect of the Atlantic."[44] These pieces added little to his fame, of course, but by this time *George's Mother* and *Maggie*, published in May and June respectively, had accumulated a number of reviews. They were generally favorable, though some voiced predictable complaints about the ugliness of poverty as an unsuitable subject for art and the "sordidness of detail" and "pitiless objectivity" of Crane's method. *Maggie*, especially, was taken by some reviewers as further evidence of Crane's genius, and for a short time was on the *Bookman*'s best-seller list.

In September the *Journal* engaged him to write a series of articles on life in the Tenderloin, and he descended once again into the big city underworld in search of materials. He sat beside a police court magistrate observing the parade of thieves, prostitutes, and drunkards, and at night he studied them in their regular haunts, unsavory "resorts" like the Turkish Parlors and the Broadway Gardens. On one of these excursions he became involved in a notorious affair that made him headline news for weeks and brought down on him the bitter and permanent hatred of the New York police.

At the Broadway Gardens one morning an hour or so after midnight, he was talking to two chorus girls about their experiences in police courts when a twenty-one-year-old prostitute known as Dora Clark or Dora Wilkins joined the group. After a time Crane and the three women left the Gardens and walked together to the corner of Broadway and Thirty-first Street, where Dora and one of the girls waited while Crane escorted the other across the street to put her on a cable car. When he returned a moment later, he found Dora and her companion in the hands of a plain-clothes policeman, under arrest for soliciting. Knowing that the accusation was false, Crane protested. The chorus girl became hysterical and identified Crane as her husband. When he confirmed the claim, hoping to help the distraught woman, the policeman released her, but proceeded with Dora to the West Thirtieth Street Station. Crane and the chorus girl followed and protested in vain to the desk sergeant. Dora was jailed, and the sergeant strongly advised the writer not to get further involved in the affair. Crane nevertheless appeared the next morning to testify in Dora's behalf at the police-court hearing, and the girl was released.

The incident was widely and circumstantially reported in the metropolitan newspapers, and Crane's testimony accusing the policeman, Charles Becker, of false arrest loosed a flood of criticism on the police. The *Journal* reported the affair under sensational headlines, describing Crane as a hero who "showed the 'badge of courage' " in risking the "censure of thousands who admire his books by manfully championing a woman of whose antecedents he knew nothing."[45] Three days after the event Crane's own full-page account appeared in the *Journal,* elaborately illustrated, and several editorials in various newspapers condemned the police. In early October matters grew worse: Dora brought formal charges against Becker for false arrest and assault, claiming that a few days after her release the policeman had approached her early one morning as she stood talking with a group of cabmen on Sixtieth Street and had brutally assaulted her, choking her, kicking her, and knocking her down twice before the cabmen finally intervened. Crane testified to the charge of false arrest at Becker's police-court trial and was subjected to a painful cross-examination by the defendant's lawyer, who accused him of maintaining an "opium joint" in his room and of habitually consorting with prostitutes. All this was thoroughly aired in the press. Crane, humiliated and angry, sent Police Commissioner Theodore Roosevelt a telegram of protest, and editorials in the Brooklyn *Daily Eagle,* the *New York Press,* and the *Journal* strongly condemned the police magistrate for permitting Becker's lawyer to abuse Crane in the lengthy, irrelevant cross-examination.

The matter ended in frustration for Crane. Roosevelt, who thought the novelist had behaved badly in testifying against Becker, ignored his telegram. Crane began two angry articles on the intolerable abuse of authority by police, but after a few opening sentences, he abandoned both, perhaps in disgust with the whole affair. A lasting consequence of these troubles was, as Lawrence wrote, "that an aroused and resentful police department bent all its unscrupulous energies to discrediting Crane and making New

York too hot for him to live in."[46] The writer did not live to see Becker's sad end. The policeman was electrocuted in 1913 for the murder of Herman Rosenthal, a New York gambler who threatened to expose Becker's connection with the underworld.

By the time the last editorial on the Becker case appeared at the end of October, Crane was getting ready for another trip for Bacheller. There seemed little enough now for him in New York. *The Little Regiment,* published that month, was bound to call attention again to his fame as a war writer and underscore once more the uncomfortable fact that he had no knowledge of real battles. When Bacheller offered him the opportunity to remedy the deficiency, he leaped at it. Cuba's revolution against Spain was now much in the news, and Bacheller conceived the idea of sending him to join the insurgent guerrillas as a war correspondent. As Crane surely realized, it would be a hard and dangerous assignment, but under the circumstances none other would have suited him better. In mid-November Bacheller issued him $700 in gold and a money belt, and the famous war writer departed for Jacksonville, Florida, elated at the prospect of seeing real war at last.

FIVE

FLORIDA AND GREECE

IN JACKSONVILLE on November 14, Crane registered at the St. James Hotel under the name Samuel Carleton, finding the alias convenient in light of his recent fame and notoriety, and set about trying to arrange clandestine passage to Cuba on a filibuster ship operating out of this city of intrigue and conspiracy. From some remote Cuban beach where the filibuster unloaded its contraband cargo of arms, he would, according to plan, make his way past Spanish patrols to the Cuban insurgents in the interior, sending out reports to Bacheller by whatever means he might discover.

He would have known, of course, the extraordinary risks of all this. In Cuban waters filibusters were in constant danger of being captured or destroyed by Spanish gunboats. Even more hazardous was the journey from the beachhead through Spanish lines into the interior. Spaniards regarded American journalists as spies and had captured several, clapping them into harsh jails to languish for weeks or months. One correspondent, twenty-three-year-old Charles Govin of the Key West *Equator-Democrat*, had suffered a worse fate. Captured by a Spanish guerrilla patrol, he had been bound with ropes and hacked to pieces with machetes.

But Crane's letters show little concern for these dangers. He wrote Amy Leslie, the beautiful drama critic of the *Chicago Daily News* with whom he had become romantically involved shortly before he left New York, that Spanish spies shadowing the correspondents "seemed very harmless" and mentioned casually that the death of General Maceo, insurgent commander in the western provinces, forced filibusters to unload cargoes on beaches further east. By early December, perhaps with the help of José Huau, an insurgent agent who engineered contraband expeditions from a cluttered back room in his Jacksonville cigar store, he had arranged passage on the *Commodore*, a large seagoing tug being readied by young Captain Edward Murphy for a run to Cuba with a cargo of guns and ammunition and a small band of Cuban commandos.

But the ship was not ready until the end of December, and Crane and other correspondents, like the dauntless E. W. McCready of the New York *Herald* and Charles Michelson and Ralph D. Paine of the *Journal*, sought whatever amusement Jacksonville offered. They loitered in waterfront saloons and hotel bars, attended the opera and theater, and congregated at the Hotel de Dream, a discreet, well-mannered brothel on the outskirts of the city owned and operated by the elegant Cora Stewart.

Born Cora Howorth in Massachusetts of cultured parents—her father was a painter—she made her way to England after the breakup of an early marriage. There she married Captain Donald Stewart, son of Sir Donald M. Stewart, field marshal and once commander-in-chief of British forces in India. But she soon abandoned the captain, perhaps because she found the prospects of life abroad in the role of wife of a colonial administrator disagreeable, and appeared in Jacksonville, where she bought the Hotel de Dream (a pun on the name of its previous owner, Ethel Dreme) and established it as the most exclusive bordello and night club in the city. McCready, years later, remembered her as "handsome, of some real refinement, aloof to most—to all, indeed, until Steve and Captain Murphy arrived. . . ." Six years older than Crane at thirty-one, the blonde, ample Cora was literary minded enough to find the dashing young writer-adventurer irresistible. Crane was surprised to find her reading one of his books, McCready said, and when Captain Murphy revealed his true identity, the news "pierced the lady's very liver."[1] The book was *George's Mother*,

Crane riding, probably in Florida,
1896 (courtesy Syracuse University)

Cora Stewart in 1892, about the time
she married Donald Stewart in England
(courtesy Syracuse University)

which Crane inscribed "To an unnamed sweetheart." As for Crane, Cora seemed to drive away whatever serious romantic feelings he might have had for Amy Leslie.

The *Commodore*, carrying a cargo of arms, sixteen Cuban guerrillas, and a crew of eleven, including Crane, sailed at dusk on December 31, 1896. Two miles downriver she ran aground in a heavy fog and was obliged to wait until daylight for the revenue cutter *Boutwell*, ironically one of the ships on station to intercept filibusters, to come up and haul her out of the mud. She ran aground again near Mayport, but dragged herself free by her own power and at last gained the open sea.

That night Crane, unable to sleep, was in the pilot house with Captain Murphy when the chief engineer came up to report trouble below. The groundings had sprung the *Commodore*'s seams, and water was rising rapidly in the engine room, threatening to overwhelm the pumps. Crane went below to help bail. The engine room, he wrote later, "represented a scene at this time taken from the middle kitchen of hades." Soapy water swirled about the booming machinery; "lights burned faintly in a way to cause mystic and grewsome shadows." The heat was unbearable, and Crane, feeling ill, came up on deck. Captain Murphy had ordered the lifeboats lowered and shortly sent the Cubans off in two of the three big ones, leaving the other and a ten-foot dinghy for the crew. When the last lifeboat had been launched, the captain and the oiler, William Higgins, joined Crane and the cook in the tiny boat and pushed away from the foundering *Commodore*. They stood off a few hundred feet until dawn, when they discovered to their dismay that seven of the crew were still aboard the ship. Their lifeboat had been stove in the launching, and they had managed somehow to reboard the ship. They had improvised rafts and put them in the water but were hesitant to jump, and Murphy shouted encouragements from the dinghy. Three leaped toward the rafts, and then the first mate, as Crane wrote memorably, "threw his hands over his head and plunged into the sea. He had no life belt, and . . . I somehow felt that I could see in the expression of his hands, and in the very toss of his head, as he leaped thus to death, that it was rage, rage, rage unspeakable that was in his heart at the time." Then the lurching *Commodore* swung wildly into the wind, rolled upright and plunged bow down into the sea, dragging the rafts and the three men on them into the maw of the ocean. Three men were still on board, leaning against the deckhouse, eerily casual, when the ship went under. "And then by the men on the ten-foot dingy," Crane wrote, "were words said that were still not words, something far beyond words." Twelve miles across the rolling sea to the west the Mosquito Inlet lighthouse "stuck up above the horizon like the point of a pin."[2]

When the laden dinghy reached the coast south of Daytona late that afternoon, Captain Murphy judged the surf too high for a landing and ordered Crane and Higgins, who were handling the oars, to take the boat to sea again, where they worked through the long night to check their drift toward the raging breakers. By midmorning the wind and current had carried them north toward Daytona, and the captain reluctantly decided to attempt to run the still-heavy surf. The boat instantly capsized, and as it went over struck Higgins, who drowned in the breakers. John Kitchell, who witnessed the scene from the beach, plunged into the surf and dragged the exhausted men ashore.

Cora, frantic since the first news of the wreck had reached her the day before, appeared shortly to accompany the exhausted writer on the train ride to Jacksonville. When he was brought into the lobby of the St. James, the haggard Crane caught sight of the nine-year-old daughter of a family staying at the hotel, an ardent admirer and dedicated autograph collector whose book he had been too rushed to sign four days before when he was about to board the *Commodore*. "Where's that album?" he called to her, and when the girl eagerly fetched it from the hotel desk, he wrote "Stephen Crane, able seaman S. S. *Commodore*."[3]

He was once again in the news. Some newspapers, like the *World* and the *Press*, gave him a prominent role in the adventure, quoting Captain Murphy's praise for his perseverance and steady courage. "That man Crane is the spunkiest fellow out," the captain told a reporter from the *Press*, which printed one of its stories under the headline "Young New York Writer Astonishes the Sea Dogs by his Courage in the Face of Death."[4] Crane's own account, syndicated by Bacheller, appeared in the *Press* on January 7, and shortly after that, working at the St. James and the Hotel de Dream, where Cora looked after him as he recovered from his ordeal, he wrote his masterpiece, "The Open Boat," finishing it by the end of February.[5]

The adventure in the dinghy was a dramatic real-life enactment of a theme that runs through Crane's work from the earliest Asbury Park reports on—the plight of man in an alien and indifferent universe. The somber sea that forms the background for the posturings of the silly summer girl and the comically vain Founder Bradley, the symbolic landscapes that envelop the little man in the Sullivan County sketches and Henry in *The Red Badge*, and the raging or empty skies that haunt the speaker in *The Black Riders* prepared Crane's imagination for this fateful encounter between experience and imagination in his twenty-seven hour ordeal in the open boat. The ambiguous seascape—"nature in the wind, and nature in the vision of men"—appears to the anxious protagonist, the unnamed correspondent in the story, in a variety of shifting, uncertain guises. It is sometimes cruel, wrathful, and deadly; sometimes beautiful and picturesque; sometimes merely indifferent. Like the hero of the poems about God and *The Red Badge*, the correspondent feels that this elusive nature is somehow the key to the mystery of existence; but unlike them he is fully conscious and introspective, aware of his solipsism and the ironies revealed by his shifting perceptions, knowing as Henry and the little man do not that this uncertainty of vision concentrates the whole baffling issue. Speaking for himself and the men, he articulates through the narrator their anxiety in face of mere seeming. To them, "the waves *seemed* thrust up in points like rocks." "Viewed from a balcony" their battle against the sea "would *doubtless* have been weirdly picturesque." It was "*probably* splendid," it was "*probably* glorious." It merely "*occurs* to a man that nature does not regard him as important." Sometimes the correspondent is in the boat, his vision exquisitely narrowed to the threat of the "slaty wall" of waves; sometimes he seems to observe their plight from afar, critically, sadly, even mockingly.

These contrasts and apparent contradictions, strikingly imaged, sustain the ironic tension in the story. To the men, the sea gulls seem at one time to be agents of a hostile nature, for "the wrath of the sea was no more to them than it was to a covey of prairie chickens a thousand miles inland." When they come close, they seem "uncanny and sinister" and "somehow gruesome and ominous" as they stare at the men with "black bead-like eyes." But another time, seen from afar, "in slanting flight up the wind toward the gray desolate east," they seem to represent not nature's wrath but nature's beauty, order, and harmony. Such ambiguities are suggested memorably in Crane's poetic language, as in the phrase "the terrible grace of the waves" and in the image of the shark, the unnameable "thing" whose "enormous fin" cuts "like a shadow through the water." Like the sea gulls, this creature strikes the correspondent as an agent of nature's inscrutable malice, and yet as he reflects, swearing dully into the sea, "the speed and power of the thing was to be greatly admired."

None of Crane's other works is as impressive in design as this artful story. Theme, image, and action are woven in fluid compositional patterns of theses and antitheses. Take, for example, the passage in which the cook, the correspondent, and the oiler discuss their chances of being rescued. The cook's assertion that they will be sighted by the lifesaving crew at the house of refuge near Mosquito Inlet is like a proposition for debate, challenged, after a balanced question and answer, by the correspondent's statement that houses of refuge do not maintain lifesaving crews. The impasse is addressed by the oiler: "Well, we're not there yet"; but the cook, unwilling to give up his comforting proposition, restates it, though allowing now for the correspondent's discrimination between lifesaving stations and houses of refuge. The passage ends with the skeptical oiler's repeated "We're not there yet." The formal design of the colloquy, with its balance and contrast of assertion and counterassertion and the refrainlike comment of the oiler, emphasizes the cook's presumption, an ironic effect amplified when the narrator intrudes to say almost casually: "It is fair to say here that there was not a life-saving station within twenty miles in either direction, but the men did not know this fact and in consequence they made dark and opprobrious remarks concerning the eyesight of the nation's life-savers."[6]

In the end, despite the apparent contradictions, the correspondent concludes that the true correlatives of nature are the "high cold star" and the desolate wind tower. The wind tower, "standing with its back to the plight of ants," seems to represent "the serenity of nature amid the struggle of the individual. . . . She did not seem cruel to him then, nor beneficent, nor treacherous, nor wise. But she was indifferent, flatly indifferent."[7] The hero of Crane's poems about God has learned this much, then, since he strutted on the "conquered" mountain, oblivious to its unconscious indifference, and desperately addressed the sky and found it filled with armies.

When Crane recovered he tried to find another way to Cuba, but by mid-March he was ready to give up. "I have been for over a month among the swamps . . . wading miserably to and fro in an attempt to avoid our derned U. S. navy," he wrote Will. "And it cant be done. I am through trying. I have changed all my plans and am going to Crete."[8] Hearst's *New York Journal* was sending him to cover the impending war between Greece and Turkey, he wrote someone else, "and if the Red Badge is not all right I shall sell out my claim on literature and take up orange growing."[9]

He was shortly in New York, rushing to settle his affairs before sailing in late March. *Scribner's* had bought "The Open Boat" for $300, but since he had lost Bacheller's gold in the surf at Daytona, Crane was short of money. He borrowed from McClure, foolishly giving him as collateral first option on his future short stories as well as the book rights to "The Open Boat." He took Linson out for a farewell dinner and told him that he intended "to marry a girl and go to England."[10] He did not mention, however, that the woman was Cora, who had sold the Hotel de Dream and was even then on her way to New York to join Crane on his journey to Greece, where she was to report the fighting for the *Journal* as "Imogene Carter," the world's first woman war correspondent. Goaded by McClure, who wanted him to start paying his debt immediately, he was hurriedly finishing a shallow adventure story, "Flanagan and His Short Filibustering Expedition," and he was too rushed to go to Hartwood and Port Jervis before he sailed for England on the *Etruria* on March 20. Cora sailed on another ship a few days later with a traveling companion, a Mrs. Ruedy, who had been with her at the Hotel de Dream. In London, the women stayed discreetly out of sight while Crane was being lionized.

He was in London four days, impressing the English literary world, as the *Critic* noted, by his "extreme and refreshing modesty." Harold Frederic gave a luncheon in his honor at the Savoy, and two days later the flamboyant war correspondent Richard Harding Davis, who was going to Greece for the London *Times*, honored him with another Savoy luncheon. Davis and Frederic accompanied him to Dover. Cora traveled separately with Mrs. Ruedy, though Davis detected her relationship to Crane and described her unflatteringly in a letter home as a "bi-roxide blonde."[11] Crane was in Paris briefly and then in Marseilles, where he sailed April 3 on the *Guadiana* for Athens, via Crete. Cora and Mrs. Ruedy traveled overland on the Orient Express from Paris to Vienna and then to Greece via Constantinople.

The *Guadiana* paused three hours at Crete, and from the deck Crane observed the fleet of the Concert of Powers, a multinational naval force occupying the harbor to keep peace between Cretan Greeks and Turks. In

Athens a few days later he wrote a memorable description of Suda Bay and the fleet, notable especially for the symbolic resonances of its naturalistic details. Over the motley crowd of warships representing the great nations of the world—a vain show of human order and enterprise—loom "exalted snow-shaped mountains," standing like the mountains of Mexico in godlike judgment on the world below them. Crete is "spread high and wide precisely like a painting [by an artist who] tried to reproduce the universe on one canvas." The distant wooded shore is "lonely and desolate like a Land of Despair." A scouting torpedo boat "as small as a gnat crawling on an enormous decorated wall" emerges from this dusky obscurity, looks the visitor over, and returns to the obscurity where nothing lives "save the venomous torpedo boat which, after all, had been little more than a shadow on the water."[12] Inscrutable nature, the pervasive air of menace, the unreachable "glory of the hills above" are among Crane's master images, tokens of a vision rising from his deepest imagination. What he actually saw in the harbor at Crete he assimilated in this splendid article into the symbolic system of his art.

In Athens on April 7, he found the city charged with war excitement. Crowds filled the streets to cheer the news of the Greek irregulars' invasion of Turkish territory in the north. Shopkeepers were locking their doors and rushing off to enlist; confidence was high that the moment had arrived to strike against the Sultan in the cause of pan-Hellenism. A letter to William written from the Hotel D'Angleterre three days after he arrived suggests that all this excitement affected Crane himself, raising in him some expectation of personal military glory. The reputation of his "poor old books," he said, had reached Greece, and certain officials had assured him that he would be offered a position on the staff of Crown Prince Constantine. "Wont that be great? I am so happy over it I can hardly breathe. I shall try—I shall try like blazes to get a decoration out of the thing. . . ."[13] He knew, of course, that such an honor would appeal to his stolid brother's high regard for status and respectability. Aware as he was of his family's frequent disappointments in his conduct, he was glad of this opportunity to present himself in a prospective role they would find admirable. But these uncharacteristic sentiments perhaps show as well what happened to Crane's sense of the grand when left unchecked by his customary deflating irony.

Turkey declared war on Greece on April 17, and Crane left the next

Cora in field uniform as a war correspondent in Greece, 1897 (courtesy Barrett Collection, University of Virginia)

Crane with John Bass of the New York Journal, *Greece, 1897* (courtesy Barrett Collection, University of Virginia)

Crane in Athens, Greece, 1897 (courtesy Barrett
Collection, University of Virginia)

day for Epirus in the northwest, where Colonel Manos was leading guerrilla attacks against the Turks around Janina. The correspondent witnessed some of this skirmishing, but almost as soon as he arrived he heard rumors of heavy fighting in Thessaly in the northeast and returned shortly to Athens. Arriving on the 27th, he found the capital in an angry mood. The Greek army had suffered defeats at Mati and Larissa and had fled south in considerable disorder and confusion to Pharsala. For these humiliations the populace blamed King George and the Crown Prince, who they felt had betrayed Greece in ordering these ignominious retreats. One Gennadius, an ambitious Athens politician, led a noisy mob to the palace to confront the King; and Crane, witnessing the scene, drew on it for one of his best Greek pieces, "The Man in the White Hat." Gennadius, the formidable revolutionary "hero of the minute," with "the mobile mouth of a poet and the glance of surpassing vanity," is met at the palace door by an old servant who declares imperturbably, "The King does not receive today." The man who wears the hat of "violence" and "terror," this "deputy of the Two-Miles-beyond-the-Extreme-Edge of the Radicals," stands there in embarrassed frustration. " 'Oh—um,' said the statesman, at last. 'Well'— He went away." Yet another irony is his reception from the roaring crowd. "As he passed through the streets his trooping followers cheered and cheered the victor, and from time to time he modestly lifted in recognition his tall white hat."[14]

Cora was in Athens by now and resolved, despite Greek advice to the contrary, to go to the front. On April 29, Crane, Cora, Richard Harding Davis, and John Bass, chief of the *Journal* staff, departed for Thessaly, traveling by boat to Stylis, arriving there in the late afternoon the following day. At Stylis they hired carriages and set out for Lamia, which they reached at midnight. Crane was listless and ill, suffering from dysentery. Finding the town crowded with soldiers, the correspondents were obliged to sleep on the floor of a "weird" hotel, as Cora noted. The next evening they were in Pharsala, where Cora hoped to interview the Crown Prince the next day. Davis and Bass went on to Velestino, Davis much relieved to be free of Cora and Crane. "He seems a genius with no responsibilities of any sort to anyone," he wrote a few days later, "and I and Bass got shut of them at Velestinos after having had to travel with them for four days."[15] Crane went on to Volo, a picturesque mountain village on the Gulf of Volo perched above a harbor crowded with English, French, and Italian warships. Denied an interview with the Crown Prince, Cora joined him there the next day.

On May 4, the Turks launched a major attack against the Greeks at Velestino. Crane lingered at Volo all that day, probably too ill to travel, but on the next day he and Cora and a Greek servant rode the twelve miles to Velestino on horseback, arriving about noon. From a mountain battery on a ridge overlooking Greek fortifications on the hillside below and the massive Turkish army in the valley beyond, Crane saw real war for the first time.

One correspondent wrote later that "the realities of war hampered Crane's imagination, his gift of picturing reality," but actually, as his descriptions of the fighting at Velestino show, he simply accommodated reality to his literary imagination. John Bass asked him as he watched the battle that afternoon what impressed him most about it. Crane cited, as Bass reported in a *Journal* article, the two radical elements of the imaginary wars of his fiction: the attitude of the soldiers and the "mysterious force" which seemed, even more than the human enemy, to be their adversary. "Between two great armies battling against each other," he told Bass, "the interesting thing is the mental attitude of the men. The Greeks I can see and understand, but the Turks seem unreal. They are shadows on the plain—vague figures in black, indications of a mysterious force."[16] These images clearly suggest variants of motifs and symbols of *The Red Badge of Courage* and other of his war stories. In Crane's imagination the black Turkish infantry surging massively up the slopes against a curtain of Greek fire and the "insane and almost wicked" squadrons of Turkish cavalry attacking against a steep rocky hill were like the black riders of the sea that had haunted him in 1894, agents of dark powers:

> These little black things streaming from here and there on the plain, what were they? What moved them to this? The power and majesty of this approach was all in its mystery, its inexplicable mystery. What was this thing? And why was it? Of course Turks, Turks, Turks; but then that is a mere name used to describe these creatures who were really hobgoblins and endowed with hobgoblin motives. . . . Anything is better than a fight with an enemy that wears the black velvet mask of distance.[17]

That afternoon or the next he watched replacement troops coming up the mountain road under Turkish artillery fire, and an incident he described in the spare, open, deceptively simple style that Ernest Hemingway is supposed to have invented shows how easily he assimilated experience to his system of metaphors:

> Reserves coming up passed a wayside shrine. There the men paused to cross themselves and pray. A shell struck the shrine and demolished it. The men in the rear of the column were obliged to pray at the spot where the shrine had been.[18]

He enlarged the passage later for the *Westminster Gazette* version of the article, adding details to the description of the shrine to enhance the characteristic theme of war as the demon destroyer of the holy order of creation, a theme memorably evoked in the famous degraded chapel scene in *The Red Badge of Courage*.

Later, in England, he would write "Death and the Child," his only significant use of his Greek experience in fiction. Like the dispatches and sketches, this fine story is another example of how real and imagined war merge in the symbolic world of his vision. The hero is Peza, an Italian war correspondent of Greek extraction who decides, in an emotional moment, to take up arms in the Greek cause. Much excited by this prospect, he works his way to a rifle pit at the front directly in the Turks' line of advance. He is dismayed, however, when the officer in charge orders him to take a rifle and bandolier from a dead soldier; he finds that he cannot touch the corpse, and another soldier is obliged to remove the cartridge belt for him. At the parapet Peza feels a rising panic. He imagines that the dead soldier's bandolier, which he is now wearing, is pulling him down "to some mystic chamber under the earth." Looking back, he sees the "two liquid-looking eyes" of a corpse staring at him, its head turned toward him "as if to get a better opportunity for the scrutiny." Peza is suddenly overwhelmed by panic. Tearing wildly at the bandolier—"the dead man's arms" —he bolts toward the rear. Far behind the lines, a tiny child, abandoned somehow in the confusion of war, finds him where he has flung himself on the ground, exhausted and despairing. "Are you a man?" the child asks, and Peza, confronting "the primitive courage, the sovereign child, the brother of the mountains, the sky and the sea," knew that "the definition of his misery could be written on a wee grass-blade."[19] The story is clearly a version of *The Red Badge of Courage*, which it resembles notably in the incident of the cowardly desertion, in its involvement of nature in the drama of self-discovery, and in its attribution of motive and conduct to faulty perception in the hero.

On May 6, the Crown Prince once again ordered a retreat, and Crane and Cora caught the last train out of Velestino under heavy artillery fire from the advancing Turks. They were at Volo during the mad confusion of its evacuation, sending their hasty dispatches to Athens by courier, and then, just as the Turks appeared on the ridges overlooking the town, boarding a man-of-war for Athens. Crane rested in the capital several days before returning to the front to cover the evacuation of the wounded from the fighting at Domokos. From Stylis he could see the dust raised by the Greek retreat toward Thermopylae, and though he was sure for a time that General Smolenski would rally his forces for a stand behind Domokos, he soon realized that the war was lost. The armistice was signed May 20, and a few days later Crane returned to Athens from Lamia, where he had gone with some vague expectation that the Greeks would make a dramatic stand at Thermopylae.

Exhausted even before Velestino, suffering still from the effects of his ordeal in the open boat and four hectic months of chasing war, Crane was too ill to travel when the war ended and was obliged to stay on in Athens, bedridden at the Hotel D'Angleterre, after most of the other correspondents had gone. When he recovered enough to walk about the glum capital, subdued and humiliated by defeat at the hands of the Greeks' ancient enemy, he went sight-seeing with the journalist Julian Ralph, who, surprised at how little Crane seemed to know about Greek culture and history, explained the architecture to him. Cora and Mrs. Ruedy, meanwhile, had departed for Paris, traveling overland via Venice, and Crane, who was to join them there, shortly began making plans to sail for Marseilles. He had added considerably to his entourage in Greece, having informally adopted two young Greek refugees, the Ptolemy twins, and a fat puppy he had picked up on the battlefield at Velestino and dubbed "Velestino the Journal Dog." He managed somehow to get them past immigration authorities at Marseilles, joining Cora and her companion in Paris. The party arrived in London about June 10. Crane must have been surprised to find that *The Third Violet*, which had been published in May,

Ravensbrook, Oxted, Surrey, where
Crane and Cora lived in the summer of
1897 (courtesy Syracuse University)

Crane and Cora, probably at
Ravensbrook, 1897 (courtesy Barrett
Collection, University of Virginia)

was a critical, if not a popular, success, proclaimed by the *Athenaeum* and the *Academy* as a book that confirmed Stephen Crane's place in the first rank of American and English writers.

He may have already decided to settle in England. It would have been clear enough to him that he could not live in New York or Port Jervis with Cora, whom he could not marry because Captain Stewart had refused to grant her a divorce. But even if he had not yet decided, English admiration and the warm entreaties of Harold Frederic, who had squired him around the clubs in London in March as if "he had invented the boy,"[20] as someone wrote, no doubt helped to sway him. In any case, he prepared to settle in England, and with Frederic's help, was soon installed at Ravensbrook, Oxted, Surrey, a few miles southwest of London, where he now entered a new phase of his career.

SIX

ENGLAND AND CUBA

FORD MADOX FORD, known then by his birth name Ford Madox Hueffer, two years younger than Stephen and years away from his own fame as a novelist and editor, was one of a group of distinguished literary people living near Oxted. Ford's cottage was in the adjoining village of Limpsfield, and Edward Garnett and his wife Constance, the renowned translator of Tolstoy, Dostoyevsky, Turgenev, and other Russian writers, lived in nearby Edenbridge. Garnett, an acute young literary critic who had discovered Joseph Conrad a few years before, would soon write an extraordinarily perceptive description of Crane's art. The burly, outspoken, unconventional Harold Frederic, whose London and New York reviews had helped spread the fame of *The Red Badge* in 1896 and who was now famous himself in England as the author of *Illumination* (published in America as *The Damnation of Theron Ware*), lived at Kenley, seven miles from Oxted, with his common-law wife, Kate Lyon. And the editor and novelist Robert Barr, who would one day be called on to finish Crane's last novel, *The O'Ruddy*, lived on a rise at Woldingham a mile or so north of the Cranes.

Crane's English reception, Ford wrote, was "tumultuous." Through his literary neighbors he met, at one time or another, William Butler Yeats, literary historian and translator Edmund Gosse, Algernon Swinburne, Henry James, probably George Bernard Shaw, and most consequentially, Joseph Conrad, with whom he established a warm and intimate friendship. Ford heard Crane talk on some military subject at a meeting of the Limpsfield Fabian Society and thought his manner arrogant and superior; but when Garnett brought him to Ford's cottage for a visit, he struck the young Englishman as altogether modest and self-effacing. Garnett queried him about his literary debt to the French realists, pointing out similarities between his method and Maupassant's. Crane denied that he had ever read Maupassant, though he grudgingly admitted that he knew one of "ol' man James's" essays on French writers. In time he came to resent such inquiries about his literary antecedents, preferring to think, rightly in a sense, that his methods were arrived at largely through intuition and free experimentation.

There had been unpleasant gossip in Greece, and Crane and Cora allowed it to be understood that they were married. The sociable, luxury-loving Cora established a lavish household, and visitors—journalists, writers, and would-be writers—came down from London with or without invitation, drawn by Crane's fame or word of his generous hospitality. He received these guests courteously and provided entertainment he could ill afford: dinners with flowers, wines, and fine foods, all bought on credit, of course, from patient local merchants. By the end of October the Cranes' extravagance, and their helplessness in business matters, had put them more than $2,000 in debt, with very little money coming in. McClure, in effect, controlled his new work, since Crane was obliged under the unreasonable terms of the publisher's March loan to turn it over to him as collateral whether McClure chose to publish it or not. His distressed letters to his New York agent, Paul Revere Reynolds, pleading for money from any source—sales, advances, or loans—give painful evidence of his reckless improvidence. "In one way Steve and I are the same person," Cora noted once. "We have no sense about money at all."[1] The trait would keep them under an anguishing burden of debt for the rest of Crane's life.

For several months England seemed ideal. His work was admired by men whose opinions he valued, and his liaison with Cora, even after it became vaguely known that she had a "past," was accepted without prejudice. "Over here, happily," he wrote an American editor, "they don't treat you as if you were a dog, but give every one an honest measure of praise or blame. There are no disgusting personalities."[2] (He did not mention Cora to anyone in America; it would be more than a year before his brothers heard about her.) But under the pressure of money troubles, the harrassment of endless visitors—"Indians" who constantly interrupted his work—and the emotional stress of enforced exile, his mood gradually darkened, and the English and their ways came to seem less admirable. "You Indians," he exploded in a letter to James Huneker, the New York music critic, "have been wasting wind in telling me how 'Unintrusive' and 'DELICATE' I would find English manners. I don't. It has not yet been the habit of people I meet at Mr. Howells or Mr. Phillips or Mrs. Sonntag's to let fall my hand and begin to quickly ask me how much money I make and from which French realist I shall steal my next book. For it has been proven to me fully and carefully by authority that all my books are stolen from the French. They stand me against walls with a teacup in my hand and tell me how I have stolen all my things from De Maupassant, Zola, Loti and the bloke who wrote—I forget the book."[3] In a poignant letter to William he blamed himself, without mentioning specifics, for his plight as an unwilling expatriate and expressed his yearning for the security of American village life. "I have managed my success like a fool and a child but then it is difficult to succeed gracefully at 23. However I am learning every day. I am slowly becoming a man. My idea is to come finally to live at Port Jervis or Hartwood. I am a wanderer now and I must see enough but—afterwards—I think of P. J. and Hartwood."[4] How Cora was to figure in this plan he did not say.

This was one side of Crane. Another was as daringly unconventional as ever. It appealed to his humor—and to something deeper than love of jest—to play the role of rough Western barbarian for the benefit of the litterateurs and intellectuals of Oxted and Limpsfield. "Superficially he was harsh and defiant enough," Ford observed; "his small, tense figure and his normal vocabulary were those of the Man of Action of dime drama—very handy in a Far Western fashion, with a revolver. He loved, indeed, to sit about in breeches, leggings, and shirt-sleeves, with a huge Colt strapped to his belt." Ford was impressed by his skill in killing flies on hot days by

Crane in his study at Ravensbrook with mementos of his Western journey on the walls (courtesy Barrett Collection, University of Virginia)

flicking them off the walls with the bead foresight, "all the while uttering Bowery variations on his theme of giving no fancy prices for antiquities." Sometimes when Frederic, Ford, and others came visiting, he demonstrated his marksmanship with his pistol. But Ford could also describe him as a "great and elf-like writer," more "otherworldly . . . than any human soul I have ever encountered."[5] There were curious contradictions in Crane's many-sided personality.

A passage in "London Impressions," which appeared in weekly installments in the *Saturday Review* beginning July 31, 1897, suggests how his observation of English life sharpened his sense of the formidable powers of cultural and social shibboleths, and demonstrates once again that curious economy of imagination which enabled him to transpose characteristic themes and tropes from one fictional circumstance to another. The legendary Far West, with its violent antipathy for conventionalized amenities and proprieties, is the antithesis of sedate London, where even the top hat, symbol of established and honored social ritual, attracts no notice whatever, even in the most plebeian of thoroughfares. Developing the point, Crane describes how citizens of Tin Can, Nevada, savagely attack a gunman who, spoiling for a fight, strolls by the saloon wearing a top hat in a bold assault on local sensibilities. Citizens of Tin Can riddle the offending top hat with bullets.[6] Such fervent reaction to social codes, taboos, and tokens is also the theme, treated in various perspectives, of "The Monster," "The Bride Comes to Yellow Sky," and "The Blue Hotel," written that fall and winter in an extraordinary burst of creative energy fueled in part by feelings ignited by his unsettling English exile.

He probably began "The Monster" at Harold Frederic's house. Injured in a carriage accident while driving to Kenley for a visit one day in August, the Cranes stayed with the Frederics for a week recovering and then joined their friends for a vacation in Ireland, where Crane finished the novelette in early September. In this acrid study of village hysteria and social cruelty, Dr. Trescott's Negro stable-keeper, Henry Johnson, is badly burned while trying to rescue young Jimmie Trescott from the doctor's burning house. Henry, carrying Jimmie downstairs in a blanket, makes his way into the doctor's flaming laboratory, where he stumbles and falls, flinging the child to safety near a window. As Henry lies unconscious under the desk, burning chemicals stream down from bursting vials into his upturned face, which by the time he is dragged to safety has been utterly destroyed. The grateful doctor saves the courageous stable-keeper's life, despite Judge Hagenthorpe's advice that he be allowed to die, and under Trescott's devoted care, Henry eventually recovers. But the faceless and mindless "monster," though harmless, arouses fear and hatred in the squeamish people of Whilomville, who come to resent the doctor for saving his life. They demand that Trescott send him to an institution, and when the doctor refuses, they cruelly ostracize him. The story ends with Trescott trying to console his sobbing wife as he mechanically counts fifteen fresh teacups set out for guests who never came.

It is easy enough to trace the major elements of "The Monster" in Crane's life and writings. The issue of moral responsibility raised by the community's dark and irrational denial of Trescott's compassion and gratitude is analogous to the issue raised for Crane by the lawlessness of the sinister Becker in the Dora Clark affair. "If you don't go to court and speak for that girl you are no man!" Dora's exasperated friend, the second chorus girl, exclaimed to Crane, who replied, "By George! I cannot. I can't afford to do that sort of thing."[7] It is the question of obligation raised, and resolved negatively, by Rose as he peers down from the wall of the Alamo into the upturned faces of the comrades he is about to desert. Crane would shortly find himself in a similar dilemma with respect to Cora, when he would decide suddenly, under the pressure of his tangled life at Ravensbrook, to abandon her to their Oxted creditors and go to war again.

The power of these commonplace themes of alienation, guilt, and obligation lies, of course, in their treatment: in the ironic revelations of a dense weave of contrasting images and ideas. Images of domestic serenity are set against images of mystical horror, intimations of generosity against cruelty, of binding convention against freedom of thought and feeling. Although the style, as many readers have noted, is closer to the norm of realism than much of his earlier work—more circumstantial, more descriptive of a broad social order than of inward states of mind—it is nevertheless richly symbolic, as the famous description of Johnson's encounter with the burning chemicals illustrates. The imagery seems in this passage to evoke a fatal and vaguely demonic impulse in nature which mocks man's fragile civil order: "At the entrance to the laboratory he confronted a strange spectacle. The room was like a garden in the region where might be burning flowers. Flames of violet, crimson, green, blue, orange, and purple were blooming everywhere." A "ruby-red snakelike thing" swims down a mahogany desk top and waves its "sizzling molten head to and fro" over the unconscious man beneath. "Then, in a moment, with mystic impulse, it moved again, and the red snake flowed directly down into Johnson's upturned face."[8]

At Ravensbrook again in mid-September, he turned once more to his Western experience, exploiting in "The Bride Comes to Yellow Sky" an idea he had broached in his 1895 articles on Galveston and San Antonio— the inevitable encroachment of communal order on the lawless legendary West. The six-gun wizard Scratchy Wilson, "about the last one of the old gang that used to hang out along the river," regularly goes on drunken sprees and shoots up Yellow Sky. Jack Potter, the cool and dependable town marshal, just as regularly restores order by facing Scratchy down. One day Scratchy goes on one of his rampages while Potter is in San Antonio secretly getting married. Wearing red-topped boots "with gilded imprints, of the kind beloved in winter by little sledding boys on the hillsides of New England" and "a maroon-colored flannel shirt . . . made, principally, by some Jewish women on the East Side of New York,"[9] the gunman strides up and down in front of the saloon, revolvers in both hands, firing at everything that moves. The marshal and his bride arrive on the 3:42, and as they round the corner of the depot, meet Scratchy face to face. Dropping the six-gun he has paused to reload, the old outlaw whips the other from its holster and flings a ferocious challenge. When the marshal declares that he is unarmed and, moreover, married, Scratchy is paralyzed with astonishment. "Married?" he stammers, noticing for the first time "the drooping drowning woman at the other man's side." Gradually the significance of the marshal's words dawns on him. "Well," he says, "I 'low it's all off, Jack." "He was not a student of chivalry," Crane writes; "it was merely that in the presence of this foreign condition he was a simple child of the earlier plains. He picked up his starboard revolver, and placing both weapons in their holsters, he went away."[10]

Scratchy, as Crane makes clear in this superb comedy, is a creation of the legend-mongering Eastern imagination, just as his costume is largely a creation of the New York garment industry. But the tragic "The Blue Hotel," which he began in December after finishing "Death and the Child," shows the dire consequences of Eastern misapprehensions about the West. The hero is a half-crazy Swede who arrives in Fort Romper, Nebraska, during a fierce blizzard, his head filled with fantasies of Western violence. He is certain that the harmless men at his hotel, painted a screaming shade of light blue, are desperadoes intent on gunning him down. In a card game with a cowboy, an Easterner, and Johnnie Scully, son of the genial hotel keeper, the terrified Swede accuses young Scully of cheating, and the two go out into the storm to fight. The Swede soundly thrashes Johnnie as old Scully and the others look on. He then leaves the hotel in triumph, pushing arrogantly through the raging blizzard, defeating it, as he feels, as easily as he defeated Johnnie Scully. In the local saloon he orders whiskey, boasting and blustering. He grandly invites the town gambler and his poker companions to drink with him. When the gambler refuses, the Swede wrathfully seizes him by the throat. There is a struggle, and then suddenly a blade shoots forward and "a human body, this citadel of virtue, wisdom, power" is pierced "as easily as if it had been a melon." The Swede crashes to the floor with a "cry of supreme astonishment."[11]

Like some of Crane's earlier heroes, the Swede is victimized by twisted perceptions and illusions created by overweening vanity. Having triumphed over the blizzard, as he thinks, he feels invulnerable to what he perceives as the violence of the lawless West and even to the formidable menace of an apparently hostile nature. "I like this weather," he tells the bartender. "I like it. It suits me." Describing the Swede's brave progress through this furious storm, Crane reflects more darkly than in *The Red Badge* on the awesome presumptuousness of this egotistical challenge to the orders of man and nature. "One viewed the existence of man [in this blizzard] then as a marvel, and conceded a glamour of wonder to these lice which were caused to cling to a whirling, fire-smote, ice-locked, disease-stricken, space-lost bulb. The conceit of man was explained by this storm to be the very engine of life."[12] Like *The Red Badge of Courage* and "The Open Boat," "The Blue Hotel" is grounded in the deepest sources of Crane's imagination, fired by his sense of man's poignant alienation in a world beset by irrational forces, the chief being man's own distorting vanity.

Under pressure of debt Crane worked steadily all that fall and winter of 1897–1898, writing besides "London Impressions," "The Monster," and the two Westerns, the thoughtful and whimsical "Irish Notes," the gossipy and trivial "European Letters" (in collaboration with Cora as "Imogene Carter"), and a number of incidental pieces, all of which he poured out to Reynolds with fervent pleas for sales and advances. "We can do large things," he wrote his agent in a hopeful mood in October, shortly after mailing off the Scratchy Wilson story. " 'The Bride Comes to Yellow Sky' is a daisy and don't let them talk funny about it."[13] But by the year's end he was less sanguine. When he sent "Death and the Child" in December, he confessed that in desperation he had gone behind his agent's back to try to bargain with McClure for an advance on his "new Greek novel," which he was just beginning. "I wouldn't have done it if I was not broke. For heaven's sake raise me all the money you can and *cable* it, *cable* it sure between Xmas and New Year's. Sell 'The Monster'! Don't forget that—cable me some money this month."[14] In January he learned that Amy Leslie, the emotional ex-actress and drama critic with whom he had begun a romance in late 1896, had got a warrant of attachment against him for $550, which he apparently owed on an original debt of $800 incurred shortly before he left for Florida. The warrant froze his royalties from *The Red Badge*, adding further to his money problems.

One satisfaction in the worrisome life of these times was his friendship with Joseph Conrad. The small, dark, temperamental Pole, fourteen years Crane's senior and still, at forty, in the shadows of anonymity, had seen in *The Red Badge of Courage* an uncanny demonstration of his own aesthetic, notably, as Conrad himself expressed it, in Crane's "gift for rendering the significant on the surface of things and with an incomparable insight into primitive emotions. . . ."[15] "Here is a man," Conrad remembered thinking as he read the war story, "who may understand."[16] Crane told S. S. Pawling, a Heinemann editor, that he wanted to meet Conrad, probably because he was then reading *The Nigger of the Narcissus*, running serially in the *New Review* that fall. Pawling invited the two to lunch in mid-October. "We shook hands," Conrad said, "with intense gravity and a direct stare at each other, after the manner of children told to make friends."[17] As Conrad had expected, there was an instant meeting of minds. They sat until four in the afternoon and then tramped through the streets of London until dusk. Conrad wired his wife not to expect him until late, and over dinner at Monico's he described in detail, at Crane's insistence, Balzac's *Comédie Humaine*, "its contents, its scope, its plan, and its general significance, together with a critical description of Balzac's style."[18] The incident stuck in his memory because Crane, as he shortly learned, was not ordinarily given to literary talk.

Crane visited Conrad at Stanford-le-Hope, Essex, in late November, taking him copies of "A Man and Some Others," a Western written in the fall of 1896, and of "The Open Boat." Conrad oddly thought the Western the better, though he found the sea story more representative of Crane's genius. "The boat thing," he wrote him, "is immensely interesting. I don't use the word in its common sense. . . . Your method is fascinating. You are a complete impressionist."[19] But in a letter to Garnett, he expressed reservations. For all the strengths of Crane's art—his sense of outline, color, movement, rapidity of action, and his "amazing faculty of vision"—Conrad felt a certain insubstantiality in his work, which often seems to flash by the startled or mesmerized reader without making a permanent impression. "He is the master of his reader to the very last line—then—apparently for no reason at all—he seems to let go his hold. It is as if he had gripped you with greased fingers."[20] In this, of course, Conrad points up the essential difference between Crane's rapid, nervous art and his own brooding, massive probing of moral and metaphysical depths. The younger writer once quarreled violently with Frederic over Conrad. The *Times* man denounced *The Nigger of the "Narcissus"* one day at lunch with several other guests at Ravensbrook (as he also, on the same occasion, denounced "The Monster"), and Crane, striding angrily up and down, shouted, "You and I and Kipling couldn't have written the Nigger!"[21] and smashed a plate with the butt of his revolver. Conrad visited Ravensbrook in mid-February with his wife Jessie, their six-week-old baby, Borys, and Jessie's sister, Dolly. The testy Conrad was amused, and also secretly annoyed, by Crane's solicitude for his three dogs, who shuffled gravely in and out of the study where the two men were writing, Crane rising with every entry and exit to hold the door for them.

He had hardly seemed to notice when the *Maine* exploded in Havana Harbor in February, but suddenly in April he was full of thoughts of war. He appealed to Conrad to help him raise money for passage to New York, dragging him about London from publisher's office to publisher's office, white-faced with excitement. "Nothing could have held him back," Conrad wrote. "He was ready to swim the ocean."[22] Finally Blackwood and Company advanced £40, for which the sympathetic Conrad gave his own future work as collateral, and within days he was gone. "I have raised the wind and sail tomorrow," he wrote in a note to a friend who lent him another £10. "Shall get myself taken in the Navy if possible."[23] He left £20 of his borrowed money with Cora, not nearly enough, of course, to settle their debts; some of his creditors, when they learned that he was gone, obtained court summonses against Cora. To escape them, and to help look after Harold Frederic, who was in poor health, she lived with the Frederics in Ireland for several weeks. When she returned to England, she was obliged to close Ravensbrook for a time and move into a London flat.

Unable to pass the navy's physical examination, Crane signed on as a correspondent with Pulitzer's *World*, which had been trying to locate him to offer him the assignment. Within days after he arrived in New York on April 21, he was in Key West, one of some hundred and fifty correspondents crowding the hotels, waiting impatiently for action. Among them were men he had known from other adventures, correspondents like E. W. McCready and Ralph D. Paine, who had been with him in Jackonsville in 1896, and the irrepressible Sylvester Scovel, who had served time in a Spanish jail in Havana and had been with Crane in Greece. As chief of the *World* staff, Scovel was in charge of Pulitzer's two dispatch boats at Key West, the *Triton* and the *Three Friends*, the latter familiar to Crane, Mc-Cready, and Paine as a filibuster tug in their Jacksonville days. Crane was the *World*'s star correspondent, rival of Richard Harding Davis of the *New York Herald* and the London *Times*, and the brilliant James Creelman of the *New York Journal*. Frank Norris, who had reviewed *Maggie* perceptively in 1896 and not yet famous as the author of *McTeague*, which he was then just finishing, was also at Key West as a correspondent for *McClure's Magazine*.

On his first day in Key West, where bored correspondents waited restlessly for the war to begin, Crane filed an empty story about the captain of the Spanish ship *Panama*, captured the day before, remarkable only for its jingoistic gloating over the enemy captain's supposed fear and discomfort. Crane and Key West seemed smugly certain that he had been a "terrible captain," strutting and boasting of Spain's might only a few days before in New York.[24] Some of his dispatches, especially his earlier ones, show that, for all his corrective irony and natural skepticism, he was by no means immune to the chauvinistic mood of the nation in those feverish times.

He was probably cruising off the coast of Cuba on a press boat in late April when Doubleday and McClure published *The Open Boat and Other Stories*, which included, besides the title story, "Death and the Child," "Flanagan," "The Bride Comes to Yellow Sky," and four other Westerns.

Heinemann's English edition, published at the same time, added nine New York City sketches, among them "An Experiment in Misery" and "The Men in the Storm." The book was received in most quarters as an important literary event. Some reviewers were uneasy about Crane's mannerisms—his preoccupation with the psychology of circumstance, his narrowly focused visual effects—and regretted his abandonment of the conventional plot involving a dramatic problem and solution; but most acknowledged him as a significant literary force, "the most striking and irresistible of all the younger American writers," as the *Spectator* said.[25]

In the first month of the war he was in and out of Key West on the *Triton* and the *Three Friends,* following navy patrols blockading the Cuban coast, waiting for the Spanish Admiral Cervera's fleet to arrive from Europe to give battle. He was on Admiral Sampson's flagship when it reconnoitered Spanish gun batteries on the northwest coast in late April, and all through May he was at sea for days at a time, roaming the Cuban coast, touching at Haiti or Jamaica to send dispatches from the cable stations there. Sometimes when the dispatch boats got in the way of the nervous warships of the blockade, they were dangerously challenged. In one of his May dispatches he described the *Three Friends'* encounter with the U.S. gunboat *Machias,* which almost ran the tug down in a suspenseful night encounter off Cárdenas. In another adventure the auxiliary cruiser *St. Paul* mistook the tug for a Spanish gunboat and chased it down in a tense race curiously like the fictional pursuit Crane had already described in his 1896 story, "Flanagan and His Short Filibustering Expedition."

He wrote ten dispatches for the *World* in May, but he was also writing fiction. Aboard the *Three Friends* he finished "His New Mittens," a story about a rebellious Whilomville lad who tries to run away from home to escape the tyranny of his mother and his Aunt Martha. This sharp analysis of the psychological maneuverings of mother and son was the predecessor of a series about the trials and sufferings of childhood, the Whilomville stories. In New York, at the insistence of a *Collier's* editor, he had reluctantly agreed to cut "The Blue Hotel" and had taken the manuscript to his room at the Everett Hotel, where he carelessly left it when he departed for Key West. He wrote Reynolds casually: "I did not get The Blue Hotel. Look it up and send it on down here. I suppose it is at the Everett." Reynolds found it there and sent it, but on May 8 Crane returned it with a curt note: "Cant cut this. Let Colliers do it themselves. Hold money & telegraph me when payment is made."[26] (*Collier's* eventually published the story in its entirety.)

Crane was not popular with some of his fellow correspondents. He seemed aloof, withdrawn, sometimes arrogant and indifferent. Richard Harding Davis wrote after the war that he was the best correspondent in the field, despite his notorious indifference to the conventional disciplines of news reporting, but Davis was often unflattering in his letters home, stating flatly once, "I do not like him myself."[27] Frank Norris, aboard the *Three Friends* on one of its cruises, once described Crane coldly as he sat in his bunk in the cabin writing on a suitcase in his lap, indifferent and faintly disreputable: "The Young Personage was wearing a pair of duck trousers grimed and fouled with all manner of pitch and grease and oil. His shirt was guiltless of collar or scarf and was unbuttoned at the throat. His hair hung in ragged fringes over his eyes. . . . Between his heels he held a bottle of beer against the rolling of the boat, and when he drank was royally independent of a glass. . . . I wondered what [readers] who had read his war novel and held him, no doubt rightly, to be a great genius would have said and thought could they have seen him at this moment."[28]

On June 10, he saw his first land action at Guantánamo Bay, where, as Crane, McCready, and Paine watched from the *Three Friends,* a contingent of 650 marines landed and established a base camp on the high ground overlooking the harbor. That evening Crane went ashore with the last marines, and the other correspondents took the dispatch boat to Port Antonio, Jamaica, to cable their stories. Paine said Crane stayed behind "because he foresaw much personal enjoyment. A hawser could not have dragged him away."[29] He was at the hospital tent several times over the next two days talking to Assistant Surgeon John Blair Gibbs, joking with him about the light Spanish resistance to the invasion. On the third night as he was approaching the hospital tent to see Gibbs, the Spaniards launched a strong and unexpected attack. Crane dropped to the ground as Mauser bullets snapped around him, but Gibbs, who had been standing in the light of the tent door, was struck in the forehead and fell forward into the dark mortally wounded. "For the moment," Crane wrote, "I was no longer a cynic. I was a child who, in a fit of ignorance, had jumped in the vat of war." Lying in the black night, he could hear the dying surgeon gasping for breath. "He was dying hard. Hard. It took him a long time to die. . . . He was going to break. . . . Every wave, vibration, of his anguish beat upon my senses. . . . He was long past groaning. There was only the bitter strife for air which pulsed out into the night in a clear penetrating whistle, with intervals of terrible silence in which I held my own breath in the common unconscious aspiration to help. I thought this man would never die. I wanted him to die. Ultimately he died." At that moment the adjutant came looking for the doctor to attend some wounded men. "Where's the doctor?" he called, and a voice in the dark somewhere answered briskly, "Just this minute died, sir."[30]

After resting a few hours on the returned dispatch boat and dictating his report to McCready, whom he scolded for ignoring adjectives and studied epithets—"Murdering my stuff," he said accusingly—he returned to the base and two days later went out with a contingent of marines to Cuzco, five miles down the coast, to destroy an enemy encampment. The unit came under intense sniper fire, and Crane was deeply impressed by the courage of signalmen who stood upright fully exposed to enemy fire while imperturbably waving semaphore messages to a gunboat off the distant coast. His superb account of the action, which the *World* headlined "The Red Badge of Courage Was His Wig-wag Flag," has been widely acknowledged as one of the best dispatches of the war.[31] He was in the fighting himself, acting as a kind of informal adjutant to the commander of the expedition, and the *New York Tribune* reported in 1900 that he was cited for gallantry under fire in official reports. In a list of notes on random topics Cora made from Crane's dictation in 1899 is this entry: "Make an Open Boat story of Cusico (?) Start where Marine went crazy and jumped over cliff killing himself, when the outpost was cut off—"[32]

As had been the case in Greece, Crane soon became ill from the rigors of campaigning, but he obsessively sought out grueling and dangerous missions. A few days after Cuzco he went ashore with Scovel and another correspondent on an expedition into the mountains behind Santiago to spy on Cervera's fleet, which Schley's Flying Squadron had bottled up in the harbor there. They rode horseback "infernal miles" through rugged woods and hills and scaled a two-thousand-foot mountain overlooking Santiago. While the exhausted Crane rested, Scovel made sketches of the black-hulled enemy warships in the harbor far below. On June 22, Crane was at Daiquiri and Siboney when General Shafter's forces landed in preparation for an assault against Santiago over the San Juan Heights. Crane and Richard Harding Davis, with the Rough Riders under the command of Colonel

Crane aboard the Three Friends *as correspondent for the* New York World *during the Spanish-American War, 1898* (Frances Cabané Scovel Saportas)

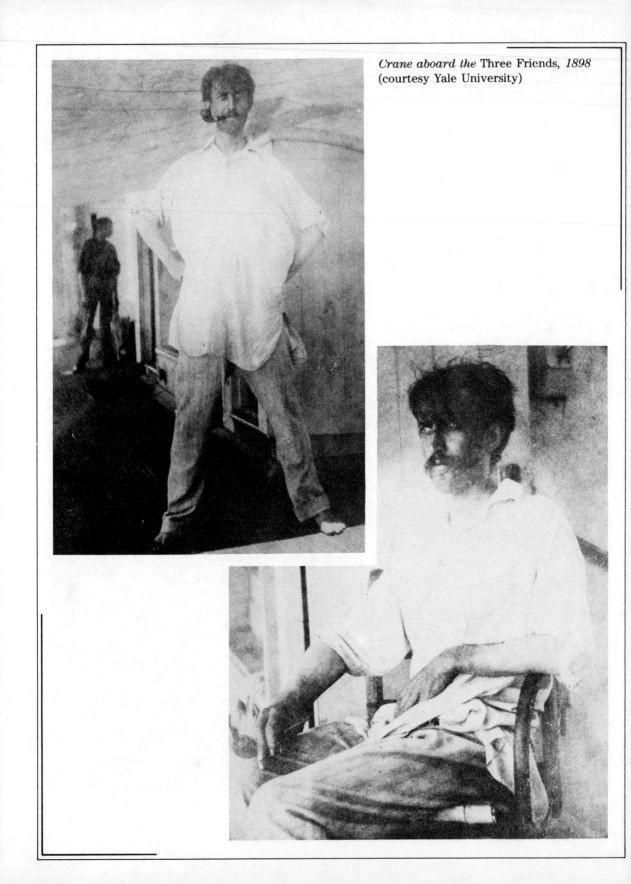

Crane aboard the Three Friends, *1898*
(courtesy Yale University)

Wood and Lieutenant Colonel Theodore Roosevelt (who ignored Crane, apparently still resentful of his role in the Dora Clark affair), found Edward Marshall, a *Journal* correspondent Crane had known since his Art Students' League days, shot through the spine and sitting propped against a tree beside the jungle trail. Crane and Davis moved him to a dressing station and then Crane took the rough jungle trail back to Siboney to notify *Journal* men there and to file Marshall's dispatches. A week later he was at El Pozo below the Spanish entrenchments on San Juan when Shafter launched his attack, and he and Davis advanced to Kettle Hill shortly after the Rough Riders captured it in their famous charge. Lying beside Colonel Wood behind an embankment sheltering them from sniper fire, Crane suddenly stood up, exposing himself and the whole unit to Spanish fire. He ignored Colonel Wood's order to take cover, but when Davis called out, "You're not impressing anyone doing that, Crane," he instantly dropped down. "I knew that would fetch you," Davis said, and Crane grinned and said, "Oh, was that it?"[33] Crane was feverish and had been deeply shaken a few minutes before when he saw an old Claverack College classmate, Reuben McNab, lying on the San Juan trail, shot in the chest. When McNab saw Crane he had greeted him by saying simply, "Well, they got me."[34]

He was in Jamaica on July 31 and when he returned was disappointed to learn that he had missed a spectacular sea battle when Cervera's fleet came out of Santiago harbor and was destroyed within hours by the Flying Squadron. He was in El Caney a day or so later where refugees were arriving in floods on the road from Santiago. The Church of San Luis de Caney was being used as an emergency surgery for Spanish wounded, and it struck Crane, who described it in the religious imagery that surfaces constantly in his work, as a powerful evocation of the dark meaning of war:

> The interior of the church was too cavelike in its gloom for the eyes of the operating surgeons, so they had had the altar-table carried to the doorway, where there was a bright light. Framed then in the black archway was the altar-table with the figure of a man upon it. He was naked save for a breech-clout, and so close, so clear was the ecclesiastic suggestion, that one's mind leaped to a fantasy that this thin pale figure had just been torn down from a cross. The flash of the

impression was like light, and for this instant it illumined all the dark recesses of one's remotest idea of sacrilege, ghastly and wanton. I bring this to you merely as an effect—an effect of mental light and shade, if you like; something done in thought similar to that which the French Impressionists do in color; something meaningless and at the same time overwhelming, crushing, monstrous.[35]

Fever and weariness of body and spirit had loosed fantasy upon a real-life enactment of sacrifice and suffering and transformed it into an encompassing metaphor of his art and vision.

Two days later, July 6, burning with fever, Crane returned to Siboney, where his colleagues Scovel and George Rhea found him and took him off, half delirious, to a medical examiner. The doctor ordered his immediate evacuation. He was desperately ill, supposedly of yellow fever. "The only fact in the universe was that my veins burned and boiled," he wrote later. He was isolated aboard the transport *City of Washington* while the ship made its slow way to the base hospital at Old Point Comfort, Virginia. But he was suffering from malaria rather than yellow fever, and by the time the ship dropped anchor at Hampton Roads on July 13, he had nearly recovered and was allowed to go ashore immediately.

Buying new clothes to replace those he had not changed in months, he went on to New York, where he found unexpected trouble. The financial manager of the *World* refused his request for an advance and disallowed $24 he had claimed in his expense account for the clothes he had bought in Virginia. The business manager, Don Seitz, charged him, moreover, with "imperiling" the *World* by writing an article criticizing the conduct of the 71st New York Volunteers in the fighting at San Juan, a story which the *Journal*, the *World*'s arch rival, loudly proclaimed as an intolerable insult to the State of New York. The *World* also charged him with disloyalty in filing Edward Marshall's dispatch at Siboney when the *Journal* correspondent lay wounded at Las Guásimas. To all this, as Seitz reported years later, Crane merely said, "Oh, very well, if that is the way you look at it, by-by."[36] He did not tell the manager that the author of the damaging story was Scovel, a fact Davis and Marshall first brought to light in 1899.

Crane signed on with the rival *Journal* to report the Puerto Rican campaign. He made a flying trip to consult a specialist in the Adirondacks about problems with his lungs, conferred with the publisher Stokes about bringing out a book of poems and a collection of Cuban war stories, and then departed hurriedly for Pensacola, where he boarded the *Journal*'s dispatch boat just before it sailed for Puerto Rico. The specialist had assured him there was no cause for worry about his lungs, but his health was not good. A colleague on the dispatch boat reported that he looked profoundly ill, much worse than he had looked at San Juan less than a month before. Covering the anticlimactic Puerto Rico campaign, he filed only three negligible dispatches. He was in Ponce shortly after General Miles landed and then in the village of Juana Díaz, which "surrendered" to him when he reached it a day ahead of the advancing army. When American troops arrived, the commander was astonished to find Crane coolly sipping coffee at the local cafe. He was in Ponce again when the armistice was signed on August 12; within days he was back in Key West, where he cabled Cora. Then, posing as a tobacco buyer, he slipped illegally into Havana and lost himself to the world.

Financially and emotionally he was near bankruptcy. His money from the *World*, perhaps as much as $3,000 all together, had mysteriously disappeared, and he was still as deeply in debt in England as ever. In September, he learned that the *Journal* had taken him off its payroll when the armistice was signed, had discontinued the payments to Cora which he had arranged for in New York, and was crediting his account, already badly in arrears, at only $20 each for his Havana articles. He had been staying at the elegant and expensive Hotel Pasaje, but he now moved, leaving a large bill, to a cheap boarding house, where he wrote steadily, day after day, in a futile attempt to stem a rising tide of debt. He wrote letters to no one, not for a time even to Reynolds, trying to insulate himself against responsibilities he was helpless to meet.

Between August and November, he wrote a score of newspaper articles, worked on *Active Service*, the novel based on his adventures in Greece, wrote several of the anguished poems on themes of guilt and betrayal in love for a sequence entitled "Intrigue," and finished four Cuban war stories for *Wounds in the Rain*, a collection of stories he had proposed to Stokes in July. Beginning in September, he sent Reynolds stories and articles in a steady stream, always accompanied by curt notes glowing with self-praise and pleading desperately for instant payment. "Now this is IT," he said in a September note sent with "The Price of the Harness." "If you don't touch big money for it I wonder!"[37] About the time he sent "The

Clan of No-Name" in October he wrote: "If I dont receive a rather fat sum from you before the last of the month, I am *ruined*,"[38] and later, "I am afraid these Journal people have ruined me in England."[39]

Cora, at Ravensbrook again, had been served two summonses, and Conrad had tried, without success, to borrow more money for her from Blackwood, offering Crane's and his future work as well as Cora's furniture as guarantees. She had been frantically trying to locate Crane and had sent a flurry of cables and letters to various officials, including the Secretary of War and the Adjutant General of the Army. General Wade in Havana eventually located him, and Crane, on money advanced by Heinemann, reluctantly left Cuba in late November. He was soon in New York, drifting and indecisive. He wrote a Mrs. Sonntag that he was trying to persuade Cora to come to New York and that she was insisting on his returning to England. "We are carrying on a duel at long range with ink."[40]

He saw Louis Senger, who remembered that he joked mirthlessly about his poor health, saying that "they had not got him yet." Senger felt that he "was essentially a soldier" who "would have elected to die in battle rather than wait for the slower death of which . . . he had a prophetic knowledge."[41] It was rumored that he had tried to commit suicide when he exposed himself to Spanish fire on Kettle Hill, and there was much gossipy speculation that he was a drunkard and dope addict. "For a mild and melancholy kid," his friend James Huneker wrote, "he certainly had fallen completely into the garbage can of gossip."[42] A policeman recognized Crane as he was coming out of a theater with Mrs. Sonntag, her seventeen-year-old son Henry, and her cousin, a priest. He tried to arrest Crane, but realized that he was with the priest, and fled.

Crane did not go to Hartwood or Port Jervis. On December 20, he cabled Cora that he was returning to England, and on December 31, 1898, he sailed on the *Manitou*.

SEVEN

BREDE

IN MID-DECEMBER while Crane was still loitering in New York, undecided about returning to England, Edward Garnett published an essay on his work in the *Academy*. It was the first major critical appraisal of his art. Taking several cues from Conrad, with whom he had often discussed Crane, Garnett defined him as a new kind of writer; and though he recognized a certain "natural limitation" in his inability to strike as deeply as some into those "rich depths of consciousness that cannot be more than hinted at by the surface," the critic declared him nevertheless to be without equal as an "interpreter of the significant surface of things." "The rare thing about Mr. Crane's art is that he keeps closer to the surface than any living writer, and, like the great portrait-painters, to a great extent makes the surface betray the depths." His method, Garnett continued, is unique: "in a few swift strokes he gives us an amazing insight . . . and he does it all straight from the surface; a few oaths, a genius for slang, an exquisite and unique faculty of exposing an individual scene by an odd simile, a power of interpreting a face or an action, a keen realizing of the primitive emotions—that is Mr. Crane's talent."[1] Years later Garnett observed that his "instinct for style" and his "psychological genius" were finally overwhelmed by the demands of journalism, the debilitating effect of his ordeals as a war correspondent, and the pressures of debt created by his extravagant and imprudent domestic life.

The last year and a half of his life was indeed a time of sad decline. His Cuban adventure ruined his already fragile health and did nothing to advance his art; the war stories of *Wounds in the Rain* flash out occasionally with the poetry and insight Garnett noted, but like most of his work after "The Blue Hotel," they show only fitfully the true powers of his integrating imagination. "The Price of the Harness," much admired by Conrad, develops a fundamental Crane theme, the virtue of courage in unfaltering performance of duty, but the theme is diluted by his topical interest in the stoical professionalism of the regular army soldier at Santiago. In "Regulars Get No Glory," a dispatch from Siboney appearing in the *World* in July, he had eloquently and scornfully protested public indifference to the quiet competency of the professional soldier, whose achievements the public took for granted, while it heaped praise on the amateurish and often self-serving exploits of the volunteer—especially on the volunteer who might bear a distinguished family name. In "The Clan of No-Name," which develops the paired themes of fidelity to duty and betrayal in love, the hero's supreme sacrifice to the ideal of duty (held dear by men of the mystic clan it invisibly binds) is played dramatically against the false standards of his status-seeking, socially ambitious fiancée. These stories, like the others in *Wounds in the Rain*, are valuable, but they lack the ironic intensity and descriptive power of his better work. Unwell and distracted by money problems, he wrote them hastily, for instant payment, using readily accessible materials and ideas. When he sent Reynolds "Marines Signalling Under Fire at Guantanamo" for McClure, he enclosed a scrawled note: "Hit him hard. Hit him beastly hard. I have got to have at least fifteen hundred dollars this month, sooner the better. For Christ's sake get me some money quick here by cable."[2]

He arrived at Ravensbrook on January 11 and found the situation there as bad as ever. The rent had not been paid in a year. A London department store was pressing strongly for payment on items bought months before, including a piano; and within a week of his homecoming, a local merchant presented him with a writ issued by a local magistrate ordering immediate settlement of an account. Cora had planned to abandon Oxted when Crane returned and had tentatively engaged another house, Brede Place, an ancient manor in Sussex near the historic town of Hastings on the English Channel. But their tangled affairs held them at Ravensbrook until their sympathetic English literary agent, the generous and long-suffering James B. Pinker, freed them by agreeing, in effect, to act as guarantor for their debts. In February, they moved to Brede with their large and growing household, which now included two of Harold Frederic's young children and their governess. (The kind-hearted Cora had taken them in after Frederic died in October and had tirelessly collected money for their support from friends and acquaintances.) There was also Mrs. Ruedy and a servant and the Crane horses and dogs. At Brede they added more servants: a butler, a cook, a gardener, a coachman, and two maids. Incredibly, their idea had been to proceed cheaply; and they had felt reassured by the fact that the owner, Moreton Frewen, an admirer of Crane's work whom Cora had met through Garnett, had made the house available to them almost rent free. But the simplest principle of economy eluded the extravagant and impractical Cranes; Cora ordered expensive embossed stationery, three hundred choice roses for planting in the front garden, and a survey by an architect, whose report was to include recommendations for repairs and restorations.

Situated a few miles from the site of the Battle of Hastings on an incline in the middle of a large park, the massive gray stone house at Brede Place is one of England's most important historical monuments. Begun in 1378 during the reign of Richard II, it was the ancestral home of the famous Oxenbridge family, who still occupied it in Queen Elizabeth's time. In Crane's day it was half in ruins. Many of its crumbling rooms were uninhabitable and there were no modern facilities: no gas, no electricity, no plumbing. It was famous for its ghosts, one of which was said to be that of old Sir Goddard Oxenbridge himself; and it had once been notorious as a refuge for smugglers and highwaymen. Servants from the nearby village of Brede refused to stay in the old house overnight.

How conscious Crane might have been of the irony of the situation— an ex-Bohemian habitué of studios, denizen of the Bowery, Western adventurer, chaser of wars, and radical individualist playing the role of lord of the manor—is not known, but Brede clearly appealed to his romantic

Brede Place, near Rye and Hastings, Sussex, where Crane and Cora settled after his return from Cuba in 1898 (courtesy Syracuse University)

Brede Place in 1858 (courtesy Barrett Collection, University of Virginia)

side. Some of his friends jokingly called him Baron Brede, and Ford
thought he took his role as Tudor lord seriously, reducing it to absurdity in
the mockery his supposed sincerity made of a "settled and august mode of
European life."[3] But if he was serious, he played his role carelessly. He
wore leggings and flannel shirts, open at the collar, and sometimes his pistol, which he strapped on when he went galloping off on one of his horses
about the park. He talked the argot of the Bowery ("I'm a fly-guy that's
wise to the all night push") and of the Western plains ("Say, when I
planted those hoofs of mine on Greek soil I felt like the hull of Greek
literature, like one gone over to the goldarned majority") and displayed
plebeian mannerisms which puzzled, and sometimes annoyed, Englishmen
—and his Anglicized compatriot Henry James, who lived seven miles away
at Lamb House in Rye.

The fastidious James visited Brede occasionally although he disliked
Cora, whose casual manners and careless, open way of talking grated on
his nerves. He was more tolerant of Crane's oddities, balancing them against
his obvious gifts. He seems to have thought of his young countryman as a
charming and extraordinarily talented apprentice, working strongly toward
a brilliant future. "We love Stephen Crane for what he is," he told someone; "we admire him for what he is going to be."[4] Ford said Crane's attitude toward The Master was "boyishly respectful and enthusiastic,"
though when James was finicky and difficult, Crane sometimes referred to
him irritably as "Henrietta Maria." They were of course worlds apart in
temperament and art, but their relationship was nevertheless one of
mutual affection and respect, even if James did think, as he told Ford, that
"the surely gifted" young man was "wholly atrocious for accent and
mannerisms."[5] Ford was also a near neighbor, having moved from Limpsfield to Winchelsea, near Rye. Conrad lived that year at Pent Farm, near
Hythe, east of Rye and not far from H. G. Wells, another member of the
literary group that centered around Rye, Winchelsea, and Brede.

These men and other friends, like the novelists A. E. W. Mason and
Edwin Pugh, were welcome enough at Brede, but within a few weeks
casual visitors like those who had imposed on them at Ravensbrook were
finding their way to Brede. Ford spoke of "tides" of "indiscriminately
chosen bands of irresponsible guests" who flowed in and out of their
sparsely furnished guest rooms. Cora had written Garnett earlier that she
hoped the "perfect quiet of Brede Place and the freedom from a lot of dear

Guests at Brede Place, July 1899. Crane is second from the left, Cora in the middle behind Crane's favorite dog, Spongie, H.G. Wells seated right, and his wife, Catherine, standing in the doorway on the right (courtesy Barrett Collection, University of Virginia)

Crane in his study at Brede, 1899 (courtesy Barrett Collection, University of Virginia)

good people, who take his mind from his work," would permit that "machine-like application which makes a man work steadily."[6] There was to be no "perfect quiet," but intractable circumstances forced a "machine-like application." Day after day that year of 1899, he sat in the austere workroom over Brede's expansive porch and wrote clever stories and novels to try to still the incessant clamor of his creditors.

In January of 1899, he had urged Reynolds to press *Harper's* to bring out "The Monster" in book form and had signed a contract with Methuen for a novel on a subject not specified. He had begun steady work on the stories for *Wounds in the Rain*, finishing all seven of those not written in Havana (including the vivid "War Memories") by the end of August. By late January, writing with amazing speed, he had also finished two new stories about child life in Whilomville, the first of a popular series that appeared in twelve monthly installments in *Harper's Magazine*, beginning in August. These charming, humorous tales reveal his natural sympathy for children and his sharp insight into the essential savagery of their inflexible social codes and conventions—and of those blindly imposed upon them by adults. By the end of March he had written three of them, when he interrupted work on the series to drive forward *Active Service*, begun at Ravensbrook in the winter of 1897 but only half finished when he returned to England from Cuba.

Although he probably conceived *Active Service* originally as a war story, it is actually an adventure-romance, a story of courtship consciously contrived for a popular audience. Rufus Coleman, a war correspondent in Greece, plunges into Turkish Epirus to rescue Professor Wainwright, who, as a consequence of the outbreak of hostilities between Greece and Turkey, is stranded there with his wife and daughter and several of his students. The sturdy correspondent finds the distressed party, which includes the professor's daughter Marjorie, whom he hopes to marry, and coolly and competently brings the group to safety. There are several interesting autobiographical allusions in the novel: the description of life at Washurst College, based on his experiences at Lafayette and Syracuse, and the descriptions of northwestern Greece, which he saw when he was in Arta briefly in 1897. The characterization of the disreputable and sexually formidable Nora Black, whose charms Coleman resists when she tries to steal him away from the pure Marjorie, doubtless refers obliquely and ambivalently to Cora. But despite brief moments in which Crane's imagination breaks through the constraints of commonplace conventionalism of the genre, the novel is an inconsequential potboiler, written, as Crane said, at the furious rate of 10,000 words a week. When he finished it in mid-May, he wrote Mrs. Moreton Frewen, wife of his landlord, a self-deprecating letter which shows that he understood its character precisely: "I must confess to you that on Saturday morning at 11.15—after dismal sorrow and travail—there was born into an unsuspecting world a certain novel called 'Active Service', full and complete in all its shame—79000 words.—which same is now being sent forth to the world to undermine whatever reputation for excellence I may have achieved up to this time and may heaven forgive it for being so bad."[7]

There was doubtless more satisfaction in the poems in his second volume of verse, *War Is Kind*, published about the time he finished the novel. They had been written over a period of several years. Some—the much anthologized "A man said to the universe," for one—were written as early as 1894, and more than half were finished before he left New York for Florida in the fall of 1896. Many are thus on themes prevalent in his writings of the time of *The Black Riders* and *The Red Badge*: man's alienation in an indifferent universe, the arbitrariness of sanctified traditions, the elusiveness of ideals, the universality of sin and guilt. The fiercely ironic title poem, the best in the collection, is a vivid evocation of violent death in battle. It was written in 1895, long before Crane had actually seen war. The ten poems in the series subtitled "Intrigue," half of which he wrote in Havana in 1898, are embarrassingly maudlin expressions of suffering in love and are intensely preoccupied with the theme of sexual betrayal and maddening jealousy, obliquely drawn perhaps from ambivalent feelings about Cora and her disreputable past.

With the novel out of the way, he turned again to short pieces, making good his promise to Pinker to flood him with stories. "If you can stick to your end, all will go finely and I will bombard you so hard with ms that you will think you are living in Paris during the siege."[8] Always the accompanying notes asked, demanded, or begged for immediate payment. "I send you a rattling good war story ["The Revenge of the Adolphus"]. . . . Please send me a checque for £40 so that I will get it on Sunday morning," he wrote in August; and again a few days later: "I must have altogether within the next ten days £150—no less, as the Irish say."[9] By October Pinker was feeling sorely tried by these demands. "I confess," he wrote,

Crane on horseback, probably at Brede, 1899 (courtesy Barrett Collection, University of Virginia)

Will Bradley cover for War Is Kind, *1899* (courtesy Barrett Collection, University of Virginia)

"that you are becoming most alarming. You telegraphed on Friday for £20; Mrs. Crane, on Monday, makes it £50; today [Tuesday] comes your letter making it £150; and I very much fear that your agent must be a millionaire if he is to satisfy your necessities a week hence, at this rate. . . ."[10] By this time, Pinker had advanced Crane a total of £230 of his own money. Reynolds, growing weary of his incessant demands and constant juggling of schemes and schedules, by July had withdrawn—or been dismissed, as Crane once hinted—and Pinker had become his agent for both England and America.

In July, he was planning a novel for Stokes on the American Revolution, enthusiastic for a while over the idea of giving his distinguished ancestors of the time, Stephen Crane the patriot and his hero sons, prominent roles; but by October he had given up the idea, fearing that the necessary research would take too much time and energy. He was also planning a new series of Westerns, though he actually wrote only two, "Twelve O'Clock" in July and "Moonlight on the Snow" in late August or September. His return to the Western materials stirred his imagination in a way the Cuban and Whilomville materials had not, and these two late Westerns, though not as intense as "The Blue Hotel" or as effortless in their comedy as "The Bride Comes to Yellow Sky," are among the best things Crane wrote at Brede. "Twelve O'Clock" describes an awesome, random explosion of senseless violence triggered incomprehensibly by the naive wonder of a bunch of cowboys who discover a cuckoo clock in the lobby of Placer's Hotel. Gathered there to see the cuckoo appear on the stroke of 12:00 noon, the cowboys are joined by a drunken gunman, Big Watson, whose angry response to a remark by one of the cowboys sets off a shooting spree that leaves three men dead in a matter of seconds. A sense of the baleful and mystic influence of random incident on human destiny, powerfully suggested in the story, is ironically evoked in the curious epigraph: " 'Where were you at twelve o'clock, noon, on the 9th of June, 1875?'— *Question on intelligent cross-examination.*"[11]

"Moonlight on the Snow" develops an idea derived from his familiar theme of the conflict between the spirit of anarchy in the legendary West and the constraining influences of commercial and civic ambition. The town gambler, Tom Larpent, "handsome and distinguished" and a "devil as cold as moonlight upon ice," shoots and kills a man who accuses him of cheating in a card game. Honoring a recent resolve by citizens of War Post to remedy its reputation for bloodshed in order to make the town fit for "theatres, water-works, street cars, women, and babies," Larpent surrenders peaceably to the newly formed hanging committee. No one in War Post wants the popular Larpent to hang. While the citizens are hesitating, pondering their dilemma, Marshal Jack Potter and his deputy Scratchy Wilson of the neighboring town of Yellow Sky ride in to arrest Larpent and take him off to Yellow Sky on a warrant for grand larceny. Thus War Post is relieved of the responsibility of choosing between civic virtue and lawless individualism.

By the end of the summer, with his financial situation steadily worsening, he was frankly writing only what he could finish quickly and sell for immediate cash. In April, the editor of *Lippincott's Magazine* had asked him to write a series of articles on great battles of the world, an assignment he was reluctant to undertake until Kate Lyon, who had been Harold Frederic's common-law wife, offered to do the necessary research. He began writing these tedious, wooden sketches from the elaborate notes she made for him in the British Museum. As he became more and more distracted by health and money problems, she gradually took over the writing herself, though when the articles were published in *Lippincott's* as "Great Battles of the World" in 1900 (and in book form in 1901), they appeared under his name alone. In October, after a quick visit to Ireland with Cora and one of their house guests, Edith Richie, he began his last novel, *The O'Ruddy*, a meandering, episodic, swashbuckling romance detailing the improbable English adventures of a quick-witted rogue of an Irishman known as the O'Ruddy. Lively with satire and ingenious burlesque, the novel celebrates its hero's inherent irreverence for authority and his sublime indifference to the pretentious decorum of English society. In writing this lighthearted *jeu d'esprit* he found welcome relief from the hard discipline imposed by critical art. When someone asked him why he should want to write a popular romance, he said, "I get a little tired of saying, 'Is this true?'" In the "long game of writing a deliberate romance," he explained, no such troublesome query is needed.[12]

He was now succumbing rapidly to the ravages of tuberculosis, malaria, worry, and overwork. Between January 1899, when he returned to England from Cuba, and April 1900, when his final collapse forced him to stop working altogether, he wrote an astonishing amount: thirteen Whilomville stories; seven Cuban war stories; the last half of *Active*

Service; nearly two-thirds of *The O'Ruddy* (unfinished when he died in June) ; two Western stories; four stories about the war adventures of the Kicking Twelfth, a regiment of the imaginary country of Spitzberg; six, more or less, of the eight sketches in *Great Battles of the World*, and more than twenty miscellaneous stories, sketches, and newspaper articles.

But there were pleasant excursions and amusements to relieve the tedium of his labor and worry. The Cranes exchanged visits with James, the Conrads, Ford, and the Wellses and played active roles in the community's social life. They often went to James's Lamb House for tea, usually taking several of their own plentiful guests, and attended such events as the annual mud-boat regatta at Rye and the charity bazaar at the rectory in Brede village. Crane was well liked, but his angular opinions sometimes disturbed the "colossal serenity" of the English. Once at Lamb House when the talk turned to the Boers and the fighting in the Transvaal, Crane drawled, "People tell me . . . a couple of [English] guard regiments could whip them in a week. When a Yankee says such things he is bragging, but I guess an Englishman is just lugging the truth from some dark cave."[13] He sometimes rode one of his carriage horses down to Ford's cottage at Winchelsea, sitting on the huge beast with "the air of a frail eagle astride a gaunt elephant,"[14] and complained about the hectic life at Brede.

Conrad and his family came for a two-week visit in June, and Crane gave their baby, Borys, a puppy named Pizanner because he was fat and square "with a leg on each corner, like an old-fashioned piano." Conrad was distressed by the number of visitors who wandered in and then wandered out to carry mean tales abroad about Cora's housekeeping. Once after a noisy bunch made its long overdue departure, Conrad remonstrated with his host for being too good-natured, and after a pause Crane said quietly, "I am glad those Indians are gone."[15] He felt curiously at ease in the company of his high-strung friend. He visited him at Pent Farm often, and the two men would work silently together in Conrad's study, where Crane sometimes lay brooding on the couch. Some of the phrases in "The Open Boat" haunted Conrad's imagination, and he sometimes quoted them at odd moments to see their effect on Crane. One day when Crane had been lying quietly on the couch for a while, Conrad said suddenly, "None of them knew the color of the sky." Crane sat up sharply, puzzled. "Don't you know that quotation?" Conrad asked. "Oh, yes," Crane said softly, and lay down again. Alluding to a passage describing waves as "most wrongfully and barbarously abrupt and tall," Conrad constantly referred to people and events as "barbarously abrupt."[16]

In July, despite his desperate financial plight, Crane took a large party to the Henley Regatta and paid all expenses. Besides the Cranes, the party included Helen Crane, William's daughter, who had been visiting since June; Edith Richie, a nineteen-year-old relative of the Cranes' friends Mabel and Mark Barr; George Lynch, a devil-may-care Irish journalist Stephen had known as a war correspondent; Karl Harriman, a young journalist from Michigan; and the novelist A. E. W. Mason. Shortly after this gay outing, Henry James came up to Brede to attend a charity bazaar, where Stephen helped Cora sell potted plants from their booth and George Lynch snapped a picture of James eating one of the doughnuts Cora had brought from the Brede Place kitchen. In September, Stephen took Cora, Helen, Edith, and the "Wild Irishman" Lynch to Paris. The party stopped over at Folkestone to spend the night at H. G. Wells's house, where they sang songs and played a game called "animal grab" until late in the evening. In the game, probably invented by Wells, everyone was an animal of some kind: Cora a chirping canary, Stephen a growling lion. On the train to Paris Crane got angry at Lynch for popping a champagne cork into a sleeping Frenchman's open mouth. While Cora and Edith waited in Paris, Stephen escorted Helen to Switzerland, where she was to attend school at Lausanne. He had to borrow money, which he never repaid, from her and from the headmistress of the school to get back to Paris. While Cora and Edith were sightseeing and window-shopping, Crane, ill with an attack of Cuban malaria, stayed in his room at the Hotel Louis le Grand to write a Whilomville story.

Conrad noted that by the fall of 1899 Stephen's life at Brede seemed often "altogether out of control." He was more deeply in debt than ever, and his health was growing steadily worse. He wrote a London friend for information about health resorts in the Black Forest. "The truth is," he said, "that Cuba Libre just about liberated me from this base blue world. The clockwork is juggling badly. I have had a lot of idiotic company all summer."[17] Talking with a young visiting journalist, he alluded obliquely to his future—or lack of one. "Yes," he said quietly as they sat in his study one afternoon, "I'm just a dry twig on the edge of the bonfire."[18] But as Wells wrote, "What he was still clinging to, but with a dwindling zest, was artistry."[19]

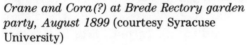

Crane and Cora(?) at Brede Rectory garden party, August 1899 (courtesy Syracuse University)

TOP RIGHT: *Cora(?) and Henry James at Brede Rectory garden party, August 1899* (Columbia University)

RIGHT: *Henry James eating a doughnut from Cora's kitchen, August 1899* (Columbia University)

Cora with three of the Cranes' dogs, July 1899 (courtesy Barrett
Collection, University of Virginia)

Cora at Brede with Spongie, 1899 (courtesy Barrett Collection, University of Virginia)

Crane at Brede, August 1899 (courtesy Barrett Collection, University of Virginia)

Cartoon showing that the stories of Crane's heavy drinking had reached England (courtesy Barrett Collection, University of Virginia)

—a dungeon into which Crane can put a publisher, should the latter prove disagreeable

THE UPTURNED FACE.

By Stephen Crane

"What will we do now? "said the adjutant, troubled and excited.

"Bury him," said Timothy Lean.

The two officers looked down close to their toes where lay the body of their comrade. The face was chalk-blue; gleaming eyes stared at the sky. Over the two upright figures was a windy sound of bullets, and on the top of the hill, Lean's prostrate company of Spitzbergen infantry was firing measured volleys.

"Don't you think it would be better——," began the adjutant, "we might leave him until to-morrow."

"No," said Lean, "I can't hold that post an hour longer. I've got to fall back, and we've got to bury old Bill."

"Of course," said the adjutant at once. "Your men got intrenching tools?"

Lean shouted back to his little line, and two men came slowly, one with a pick one with a shovel. They started in the direction of the Rostina sharp-shooters. Bullets cracked near their ears. "Dig here," said Lean gruffly. The men, thus caused to lower their glances to the turf, became hurried and frightened merely because they could not look to see whence the bullets came. The dull heat of the pick striking the earth sounded amid the swift snap of close bullets. Presently the other private began to shovel.

"I suppose," said the adjutant, slowly, "we'd better search his clothes for—things."

Lean nodded; together in curious abstraction they looked at the body. Then Lean stirred his shoulders suddenly, arousing himself.

First page of "The Upturned Face," which Crane sent to his agent in November 1899 (courtesy Barrett Collection, University of Virginia)

Caricature of Crane punishing a publisher at Brede, (Saturday Evening Post, April 1899)

In November Crane sent Pinker a tiny masterpiece, "The Upturned Face." Two unnerved young officers of a company of Spitzbergen infantry are burying a fallen comrade in an open field under enemy sharpshooter fire. Old Bill's corpse, its face "chalk-blue," looks keenly out of a shallow grave, its gleaming eyes staring at the sky. The officers cannot remember the burial service. Bullets snap and whistle through the air over their heads. The adjutant pathetically tries a beginning:

> "*O, God, have Mercy*—"
> "*O, God, have Mercy*—" said Lean.
> " '*Mercy*,' " repeated the adjutant in a quick failure.
> " '*Mercy*,' " said Lean.

Lean cannot throw dirt on the ghastly face. He throws in shovel after shovel of earth, each throw "like a gesture of abhorrence," but never on the face. "Good God," he cries to the adjutant. "Why didn't you turn him somehow when you put him in? This—" The adjutant's lips are white. "Go on man," he shouts beseechingly. Lean swings the shovel in a pendulum arc. When the earth falls it makes a sound—plop.[20]

In its precision and perfect economy, its flawless representation of the gesture, posture, and inarticulate speech of extreme mental distress, this harrowing story is as good as anything he ever wrote, and he knew it. "I am enclosing a double extra special good thing," he wrote Pinker. "I will not disguise from you that I am wonderfully keen on this small bit of 1500 words."[21] He was "almost" tempted, he said, to ask Pinker to place it in the best rather than in the best-paying magazine, evidence of a remarkable faith considering his intolerable financial state.

He was in good spirits in November despite his troubles, and some of his old delight in the absurd showed in his plans for an elaborate Christmas and New Year's celebration party at Brede. "We of Brede Place," he wrote the novelist H. B. Marriott-Watson, "are giving a free play to the villagers at Chritmas time in the school-house and I have written some awful rubbish which our friends will on that night speak out to the parish." The "awful rubbish" was his play "The Ghost," an inane farce he had conceived to honor the chief ghost of Brede, and his plan was to invite his famous literary friends—"a terrible list of authors," a truly "distinguished rabble"—to contribute to its composition. "I have asked Henry James,

Robert Barr, Joseph Conrad, A. E. W. Mason, H. G. Wells, Edwin Pugh, George Gissing, Rider Haggard and yourself to write a mere word—any word 'it,' 'they,' 'you,'—any word and thus identify themselves with this crime."[22] Conrad sent in the line "This is a jolly cold world" and Crane worked it and other such contributions into the preposterous plot. The music, which the Wellses apparently managed, was stolen from *The Mikado* and *Pinafore*. The party was to last three days. Cora engaged extra servants and invited thirty or forty guests, renting beds and cots for them from the local hospital. The house was elaborately decorated, and for the banquet the cooks prepared forty flaming plum puddings.

The play was performed at Brede schoolhouse on December 28 during a violent snowstorm, which continued through the next day. Bad weather kept the villagers away from the ball the next evening, and the houseguests amused themselves by playing stickhorse (another of H. G. Wells's improvised games) and poker, with Crane as instructor. He seemed unusually quiet and withdrawn. Wells described him as a "lean, blond, slow-speaking, perceptive, fragile, tuberculous being, too adventurous to be temperate with anything and impracticable to an extreme degree. . . . He was profoundly weary and ill, if I had been wise enough to see it, but I thought him sulky and reserved."[23] After the party one of the guests wandering through the old house found him sitting alone with his face close to a guitar as he softly plucked a single string. When the guest approached him, Crane fainted against his shoulder. During the night he had a severe hemorrhage, and Wells rode off on a bicycle to Rye in the wintry dawn to fetch a doctor.

He recovered enough in early January of 1900 to work on *The O'Ruddy* and the Lippincott battle articles. Cora wrote Pinker almost daily begging funds, offering schemes, pleading, while Crane worried about advances on the novel. On January 2 Cora apologized to Pinker for her incessant demands for money and assured him that Crane would one day "prove his appreciation of your simply saving him from going smash."[24] But three days later Crane wrote him a brutal and irrational letter:

> I must have the money. I cannot get on without it. If you cannot send £50 by the next mail, I will have to find a man who can. I know this is abrupt and unfair, but self-preservation forces my game with you precisely as it did with Reynolds.[25]

Pinker telegraphed an indignant protest, and Cora assured him at once that Crane had intended no threat and was quite "upset" by his response. Pinker took this as an apology, and Crane wrote immediately: "I hardly know what to say further save that you are a BENIFIT [*sic*]."[26] He worked on the romance and the battle articles Kate Lyon was drafting—or writing—for him. His nerves were bad, and he was not as good-natured about his unwelcome guests as he had once been—"lice," he called them. Once he lashed out in a note: "Please have the kindness to keep your mouth shut about my health in front of Mrs. Crane hereafter. She can do nothing for me and I am too old to be nursed. It is all up with me but I will not have her scared. For some funny woman's reason, she likes me. Mind this."[27]

Cora was in Paris in early April helping Helen Crane shop for clothes when she received a telegram from Brede with the news that Crane had suffered two massive hemorrhages. Returning immediately to England, she ordered a great specialist from London, who examined him at Brede and charged £50 for his opinion that his condition was not serious. The hemorrhaging stopped, but Crane was getting weaker every day, suffering by late April from an abscess in the bowels and recurrent attacks of malaria. The doctors were certain he would recover, and Crane was encouraged to plan a sea voyage and consider a move to Texas for the benefits of its climate. The Cranes at Port Jervis and Hartwood followed the daily bulletins on his condition in the New York papers, which were more optimistic than hard facts warranted. In late April, Cora began making arrangements to move him to a sanitarium at Badenweiler in the Black Forest. Moreton Frewen and Walter Goode, a journalist friend, raised £150 for the journey, most of it from J. P. Morgan and Andrew Carnegie. The entourage Cora assembled was certainly expensive enough; besides Helen, it included the Brede butler, and Crane's favorite dog Sponge, two nurses, and a doctor. Shortly before they left Brede, Crane sent a dictated note to an influential friend asking him to try to help Conrad, who was ill and discouraged. "I have Conrad on my mind very much just now. . . . He is poor and a gentleman and proud. . . . If Garnett should ask you to help pull wires for a place on the Civil List for [him] please do me the last favor. . . ."[28] This was Crane's last letter.

At the fashionable Lord Warden Hotel in Dover, where they paused several days, Crane's room looked out over the English Channel. He spent

Last photograph of Crane, with Spongie, spring 1900
(courtesy Barrett Collection, University of Virginia)

Crane's grave in Hillside, New Jersey

hours gazing at the sailboats and contemplating, Wells thought, his old adversary. Wells came from Folkestone for a visit. Conrad, who came a day or two later, was shocked at his haggard appearance. Robert Barr, at Cora's request, came and stayed four days to take notes on Crane's whispered instructions for the completion of *The O'Ruddy*, which he got Barr to promise to finish. On May 24, the entourage departed for Germany, stopping over for a day or so at Basel, and arriving at the sanitarium in Baden-weiler on the 27th. The money Frewen had raised was by now exhausted, and Cora wrote a frantic letter to Pinker pleading funds. Frewen sent £25 and Henry James sent, as a token of his "tender benediction," a check for £50. By June 3, Crane's mind had become cloudy, and he seemed tormented by feverish dreams. "My husband's brain is never at rest," Cora wrote Frewen. "He lives over everything in dreams and talks aloud constantly. It is too awful to hear him try to change place in the *Open Boat*!"[29] At three o'clock in the morning on June 5, 1900, he died.

His body was on view at a London mortuary for a week, and in mid-June Cora and Helen accompanied it to New York. The Reverend Dr. Buckley, an old friend of the Crane family, preached the funeral sermon, saying that Stephen's career had been "like that of a meteor which gleams brilliantly in the sky for a time and then sinks to rest."[30] He was buried in the Evergreen Cemetery at Hillside, New Jersey, under a headstone marked: "Stephen Crane—Poet—Author—1871–1900."

AFTER VISITING the Crane family at Port Jervis, Cora returned to London, where she tried without success to earn her living as a free-lance writer. Finding no buyers for her own stories, she concocted endings for several Stephen had left unfinished, among them "The Squire's Madness" and "The Man from Duluth." She arranged for the publication of *Last Words*, a volume of odds and ends from Crane's papers published in 1902, but neither this nor *The O'Ruddy*, which Robert Barr finally finished in 1903, lifted the burden of debt—nearly five thousand dollars—that Crane had left her. She returned to her own country in 1901, eventually drifting back to Jacksonville and the social underworld she had abandoned to follow Crane to Greece in 1897. In 1902, she borrowed from friends and local bankers and built an elegant brothel she named The Court, which she presided over with the same flair she had shown as the madam of the Hotel de Dream. She married Hammond McNeil, a blacksheep son of a prominent

Georgia family nearly fifteen years her junior, who later accused her of an adulterous affair and who in 1907—in a sensational shooting Cora witnessed—murdered the man he suspected was her lover. She left for England shortly before McNeil's trial to avoid testifying. She called on the Conrads, the Wellses, and the Frewens; but Henry James declined to see her, sending a curt note saying that he planned to be in London and that "a call at Lamb House will not find yours truly." She returned to Jacksonville after McNeil was acquitted, but the scandalous affair marked the beginning of her decline in popularity as a hostess. She was shunned in her last years by many who had been flattered to know her in her heyday as a flamboyant demimondaine. She died of a stroke in 1910 at the age of forty-five and was buried in Jacksonville as Cora E. Crane.

NOTES

INTRODUCTION

1. Joseph Conrad to Stephen Crane, 1 December 1897, Letter 210, *Stephen Crane: Letters*, ed. R. W. Stallman and Lillian Gilkes (New York: New York University Press, 1960), 154.

2. H. G. Wells, "Stephen Crane from an English Standpoint," *North American Review* 171 (August 1900): 242.

3. Joseph Conrad to Peter F. Somerville, [1912?], Letter 16, app., *Letters*, 322.

4. Quoted by R. W. Stallman, *Stephen Crane: A Critical Bibliography* (Ames: Iowa State University Press, 1972), 297.

5. Edward Garnett, "Stephen Crane and His Work," in *Friday Nights: Literary Criticism and Appreciations* (New York: Knopf, 1922), 213–14; reprinted in Thomas A. Gullason, ed., *Stephen Crane's Career: Perspectives and Evaluations* (New York: New York University Press, 1972), 143.

6. H. L. Mencken, Introduction to *Major Conflicts*, vol. 10 of *The Work of Stephen Crane*, ed. Wilson Follett (New York: Knopf, 1925–27), ix–xiii.

7. Arthur Hobson Quinn, *American Fiction: An Historical and Critical Study* (New York: Appleton-Century, 1936), 532–38.

8. Fred L. Pattee to Alfred A. Knopf, 19 December 1939, quoted by R. W. Stallman, *Stephen Crane: A Critical Bibliography*, 353.

ONE: THE PARSONAGE

1. Quoted in *Stephen Crane's Career: Perspectives and Evaluations*, ed. Thomas A. Gullason (New York: New York University Press, 1972), 20.
2. Crane to the editor of the *Newark Sunday Call*, 29 April 1896, Letter 159, *Stephen Crane: Letters*, ed. R. W. Stallman and Lillian Gilkes (New York: New York University Press, 1960), 124. Cited hereafter as *Letters*.
3. Frederic M. Lawrence, *The Real Stephen Crane*, ed. Joseph Katz (Newark, N.J.: Newark Public Library, 1980), 14.
4. Crane to Nellie Crouse, 11 February [1896], Letter 144, *Letters*, 115.
5. George H. Genzmer, "Jonathan Townley Crane," in *Dictionary of American Biography*, ed. Allen Johnson and Dumas Malone (New York: Scribner's, 1930), 6.
6. Crane to Willis B. Clarke, [November 1899], Letter 314, *Letters*, 243.
7. Crane to John Northern Hilliard, 2 January [1896], Letter 125, *Letters*, 94.
8. Crane to Willis B. Clarke, [November 1899], Letter 314, *Letters*, 242.
9. Ibid., 241.
10. Ibid., 242.
11. Helen R. Crane, "My Uncle, Stephen Crane," *American Mercury* 31 (January 1934): 25.
12. Melvin Schoberlin, Introduction to *The Sullivan County Sketches of Stephen Crane* (Syracuse, N.Y.: Syracuse University Press, 1949), 3.
13. Corwin K. Linson, *My Stephen Crane*, ed. Edwin H. Cady (Syracuse, N.Y.: Syracuse University Press, 1958), 6.
14. Crane to Willis B. Clark, [November 1899], Letter 314, *Letters*, 243.
15. Ibid.
16. Crane to an editor of *Leslie's Weekly*, [ca. November 1895], Letter 111, *Letters*, 78.
17. "I'd Rather Have—" in *Poems and Literary Remains*, vol. 10 of *The Works of Stephen Crane*, 10 vols., ed. Fredson Bowers (Charlottesville: The University Press of Virginia, 1975), 73. Cited hereafter as *Works*.
18. Post Wheeler and Hallie Ermine Rives, *Dome of Many-Coloured Glass* (New York: Doubleday, 1955), 21.
19. Crane to Willis B. Clarke, [November 1899], Letter 314, *Letters*, 242.
20. Ibid.
21. Thomas A. Gullason, "The Cranes at Pennington Seminary," *American Literature* 39 (January 1968): 540.
22. Thomas Beer, *Stephen Crane: A Study in American Letters* (New York: Knopf, 1927), 52.

23. Harvey Wickham, "Stephen Crane at College," *American Mercury* 7 (March 1926) : 291–92.
24. Beer, 53.
25. Wickham, 294.
26. Crane to Viola Allen, 15 March 1896, Letter 150, *Letters*, 119.
27. Wickham, 293.
28. Ibid., 295.
29. Ibid., 296.
30. Ibid., 295.
31. *The Vidette* (May 1890), 11. Also in *Works*, vol. 8, 567.
32. "Mr. Yatman's Conversions," *New York Tribune*, 27 Aug. 1888, 2. Also in *Works*, vol. 8, 531.
33. Clarence N. Goodwin, who knew Crane at Syracuse University. Quoted by R. W. Stallman, *Stephen Crane: A Critical Bibliography* (Ames: Iowa State University Press, 1972), 332.
34. Quoted by David E. Sloane, "Stephen Crane at Lafayette," *Resources for American Literary Study* 2 (Spring 1972), 104.
35. Ernest G. Smith, who knew Crane at Lafayette College. Quoted by Lyndon U. Pratt, "The Formal Education of Stephen Crane," *American Literature* 10 (1939) : 469, n. 43.
36. Crane to John Northern Hilliard, 2 January [1896], Letter 125, *Letters*, 94.
37. Crane to an editor of *Leslie's Weekly*, [ca. November 1895], Letter 111, *Letters*, 78.
38. Crane to Odell Hathaway, 9 January 1891, Letter 6, *Letters*, 8.
39. Frank Noxon to Max J. Herzberg, 7 December 1926, Letter 24, app., *Letters*, 334.
40. Mansfield J. French, "Stephen Crane, Ball Player," *Syracuse University Alumni News* 15 (January 1934) : 3.
41. Frank Smalley to Cora Crane, 2 August 1900, Letter 7, app., *Letters*, 307.
42. Beer, 205.
43. Crane to the Reverend Charles Little, 6 February 1899, Letter 268, *Letters*, 208–9.
44. Wickham, 292.
45. French, 3.
46. Lawrence, 4.
47. *Works*, vol. 8, 578–80.
48. Crane to John Northern Hilliard, [ca. January 1896], Letter 137, *Letters*, 108–9.

TWO: ASBURY PARK

1. Ralph D. Paine, *Roads of Adventure* (New York: Houghton Mifflin, 1922), 162–63.
2. "Asbury Park's Big Board Walk," *New York Tribune*, 30 Aug. 1890, 13. Also in *Works*, vol. 8, 543.
3. "Gay Bathing Suit and Novel Both Must Go," *New York Tribune*, 5 Aug. 1888. Quoted by Victor Elconin in "Stephen Crane at Asbury Park," *American Literature* 20 (November 1948) : 276.
4. "The Rise of Ocean Grove," *New York Tribune*, 17 Aug. 1889. Quoted by Elconin, 275.
5. M[ary] H[elen] Crane, "Change of Base," *Ocean Grove Record*, 15 Mar. 1884, 3; reprinted in Gullason, *Stephen Crane's Career*, 36.
6. Arthur Oliver, "Jersey Memories—Stephen Crane," *Proceedings of the New Jersey Historical Society* 16 (October 1931) : 461.
7. "Asbury Park," *New York Tribune*, 24 Aug. 1890, 13. Also in *Works*, vol. 8, 541.
8. "Avon's School by the Sea," *New York Tribune*, 4 Aug. 1890, 5. Also in *Works*, vol. 8, 503.
9. Ibid. Also in *Works*, vol. 8, 502–3.
10. "Arriving at Ocean Grove," *New York Tribune*, 29 June 1891, 5. Also in *Works*, vol. 8, 546.
11. "On the Banks of Shark River," *New York Tribune*, 11 July 1891, 5. Also in *Works*, vol. 8, 548–49.
12. "The Wreck of the *New Era*," *Connecticut Campus Fine Arts Magazine*, 28 April 1956, 1–2, 19–20. Also in *Works*, vol. 8, 580–84.
13. "Apache Crossing," *Works*, vol. 10, 99–100.
14. Hamlin Garland, "Stephen Crane: A Soldier of Fortune," *Saturday Evening Post*, 16 August 1900, 16; reprinted in *Letters*, 300.
15. Eugène Véron, *Aesthetics*, trans. W. H. Armstrong (Philadelphia: Lippincott; London: Chapman and Hall, 1879), xxii, xxiv.
16. "Ibsen as Dramatist," *Arena* 2 (June 1890) : 72.
17. Oliver, 454.
18. Rudyard Kipling, *The Light That Failed*, vol. 9 of *The Writings in Prose and Verse* (New York: Scribner's, 1909), 53.
19. Lawrence, 4.
20. All quotations in this paragraph are from Beer, 60–64; reprinted in *Letters*, 9–10.
21. Crane to Acton Davies, [26 May 1892], Letter 12, *Letters*, 11.
22. "Hunting Wild Hogs," *New York Tribune*, 28 Feb. 1892, 17. Also in *Works*, vol. 8, 202.

23. *Works*, vol. 10, 100–104.
24. "On the Boardwalk," *New York Tribune*, 14 Aug. 1892, 17. Also in *Works*, vol. 8, 515.
25. "Meetings Begun at Ocean Grove," *New York Tribune*, 2 July 1892, 4. Also in *Works*, vol. 8, 508.
26. "Crowding into Asbury Park," *New York Tribune*, 3 July 1892, 28. Also in *Works*, vol. 8, 510.
27. "Summer Dwellers at Asbury Park and Their Doings," *New York Tribune*, 24 July 1892, 22. Also in *Works*, vol. 8, 514.
28. "On the Boardwalk," 517.
29. Ibid., 517, 518.
30. Ibid., 518.
31. Ibid., 518–19.
32. The other tales were "A Ghoul's Accountant," "The Black Dog," and "Killing His Bear," which appeared in July with two articles on Sullivan County.
33. "Four Men in a Cave," *Works*, vol. 8, 225.
34. "The Mesmeric Mountain," *Works*, vol. 8, 268. First published in **Last Words** (1902).
35. "The Black Dog," *Works*, vol. 8, 242.
36. "A Ghoul's Accountant," *Works*, vol. 8, 240.
37. "The Octopush," *Works*, vol. 8, 231.
38. *Works*, vol. 5, 3.
39. "Parades and Entertainments, *New York Tribune*, 21 Aug. 1892, 22. Also in *Works*, vol. 8, 521, 522.
40. Crane to Lily Brandon Munroe, [ca. March 1894], Letter 34, *Letters*, 31.
41. Ibid., 31–32.
42. Crane to William Dean Howells, 17 Aug. 1895, Letter 80, *Letters*, 62.

THREE: NEW YORK
1. Lawrence, 6, 7–8.
2. Beer, 87.
3. Ibid., 82.
4. Quoted in *Letters*, 11, n. 11.
5. Helen R. Crane, "My Uncle, Stephen Crane," 25.
6. *Writings*, vol. 9, 41.
7. Crane to an editor of *Leslie's Weekly*, [ca. November 1895], Letter 111, *Letters*, 78–79.
8. *Works*, vol. 6, 254.
9. *Works*, vol. 10, 87.
10. Corwin K. Linson, 31.

11. Ibid., 30.
12. Willis Fletcher Johnson, "The Launching of Stephen Crane," *Literary Digest International Book Review* 4 (April 1926) : 289.
13. Beer, 90–91.
14. Frank Norris, "Stephen Crane's Stories of Life in the Slums," *Wave* (San Francisco) 15 (4 July, 1896) : 13.
15. T. D. Talmage, *The Masque Torn Off* (Chicago: Fairbanks, Palmer, 1882), 65.
16. "Deplorable Social Conditions," *Arena* 15 (February 1891) : 375.
17. Albert Ross, "What Is Immoral in Literature," *Arena* 15 (March 1891) : 439.
18. John Berryman, *Stephen Crane* (New York: William Sloane, 1950), 52.
19. *Works*, vol. 1, 11.
20. Norris, 13.
21. Hamlin Garland, "Stephen Crane: A Soldier of Fortune," *Saturday Evening Post*, 28 July 1900, 16.
22. John D. Barry to Stephen Crane, 22 March 1893, *Stephen Crane Newsletter* 2, no. 1 (Fall 1967) : 1–3.
23. Linson, 33.
24. Crane to Holmes Bassett, [ca. March 1893], Letter 19, *Letters*, 15.
25. Crane to Miss Wortzmann, [ca. March 1893], Letter 20, *Letters*, 15.
26. Crane to William Dean Howells, 28 March 1893, Letter 23, *Letters*, 16.
27. William Dean Howells to Cora Crane, 29 July 1900, Letter 6, app., *Letters*, 306.
28. Beer, 99.
29. Crane to Lily Brandon Munroe, [ca. April 1893], Letter 28, *Letters*, 20–21.
30. Johnson, 289.
31. Crane to an editor of *Leslie's Weekly*, [ca. November 1895], Letter 111, *Letters*, 79.
32. Lawrence, 10.
33. *Works*, vol. 8, 33.
34. Louis C. Senger to Hamlin Garland, 9 October 1900, Letter 12 app., *Letters*, 319.
35. Crane to Mrs. Armstrong, [2 April 1893], Letter 25, *Letters*, 17.
36. Linson, 37.
37. Frederic G. Gordon to Thomas Beer, 25 May 1923, Letter 20, app., *Letters*, 330. See also Crane, "The Art Students' League Building," *Works*, vol. 8, 315.
38. David Ericson to Ames W. Williams, 4 November 1942, Letter 26, app., *Letters*, 341.
39. *Works*, vol. 1, 20.
40. "A Great Mistake," *Works*, vol. 8, 50.

41. *Works*, vol. 8, 52.
42. *Works*, vol. 8, 50.
43. Linson, 19.
44. Garland, Hamlin, "An Ambitious French Novel and a Modest American Story," *Arena* 8 (June 1893) : xi–xii.
45. Linson, 51.
46. *Works*, vol. 10, 5.
47. Hamlin Garland, *Roadside Meetings* (New York: Macmillan, 1930), 193–95.
48. Linson, 50.
49. *Works*, vol. 10, 8.
50. *Works*, vol. 10, 23.
51. *Works*, vol. 10, 41.
52. *Works*, vol. 10, 21.
53. *Works*, vol. 10, 13.
54. *Works*, vol. 10, 53.
55. Linson, 51–52.
56. Quoted by Linson from the *New York Tribune*, 16 April 1894, in *My Stephen Crane*, 56.
57. Linson, 56.
58. *Works*, vol. 8, 283.
59. *Works*, vol. 8, 315.
60. Crane to Catherine Harris, [ca. 12 November 1896], Letter 178, *Letters*, 133.
61. Crane to Hamlin Garland, [ca. 18 April 1894], Letter 35, *Letters*, 35.
62. Garland, *Roadside Meetings*, 196.
63. *Works*, vol. 2, 46–48.
64. Ibid., 38.
65. Ibid., 82.
66. Garland, *Roadside Meetings*, 196.
67. "The Gratitude of a Nation," *Works*, vol. 8, 589.
68. *Works*, vol. 8, 58. Crane titled the piece "An Excursion Ticket" in a pasteup of the *New York Press* clipping.
69. *Letters*, 36.
70. *Works*, vol. 8, 590.
71. Crane to Copeland and Day, 9 September 1894, Letter 43, *Letters*, 39–40.
72. Frederic Gordon to Copeland and Day, [ca. January 1895], Letter 57, *Letters*, 48.
73. Howells to Crane, 2 October 1894, Letter 44, *Letters*, 40.
74. *Works*, vol. 8, 304.
75. *Works*, vol. 8, 309.
76. *Works*, vol. 8, 324, 326.

77. "Stories Told by an Artist," *Works*, vol. 8, 68, and "The Silver Pageant," *Works*, vol. 8, 76.

78. *Works*, vol. 8, 338.

79. *Works*, vol. 8, 345.

80. Crane to Hamlin Garland, 15 November, [1894], Letter 46, *Letters*, 41.

81. Irving Bacheller to Cora Crane, 13 July 1900, Letter 4, app., *Letters*, 298.

82. Crane to Hamlin Garland, 15 November, [1894], Letter 46, *Letters*, 41.

83. "Howells Fears Realists Must Wait," *New York Times*, 28 October 1894, 20. Also in *Works*, vol. 8, 638.

84. *Works*, vol. 1, 129.

85. "Realism and a New Realist," *Philadelphia Press*, 8 December 1894, 7; reprinted in R. M. Weatherford, *Stephen Crane: The Critical Heritage* (Boston: Routledge & Kegan Paul, 1973), 82–83.

86. Crane to Ripley Hitchcock, 18 December 1894, Letter 50, *Letters*, 46.

87. Crane to Copeland and Day, [6 January and 10 January 1895], Letters 53, 54, *Letters*, 47.

88. Crane to Ripley Hitchcock, [ca. 30 January 1895], Letter 60, *Letters*, 49.

89. Crane to Ripley Hitchcock, [ca. 12 February 1895], Letter 61, *Letters*, 51.

FOUR: THE WEST, MEXICO, AND NEW YORK

1. Willa Cather, "When I Knew Stephen Crane," *Prairie Schooner*, 23 (Fall 1949): 233.

2. "Nebraska's Bitter Fight for Life," *Works*, vol. 8, 416, 417–18.

3. Ibid., 409–15.

4. *Works*, vol. 5, 158.

5. Cather, 235.

6. *Works*, vol. 8, 82.

7. Crane to Corwin K. Linson, [19 February 1895], Letter 63, *Letters*, 52.

8. *Works*, vol. 8, 459.

9. Crane to Ripley Hitchcock, 8 March 1895, Letter 66, *Letters*, 53.

10. "Galveston, Texas, in 1895," *Works*, vol. 8, 474–75.

11. "Stephen Crane in Texas," *Works*, vol. 8, 472.

12. Crane to Edward Grover, [March ? 1895], Letter 67, *Letters*, 54.

13. Crane to Dr. Lucius L. Button, 12 March 1895, Letter 68, *Letters*, 54–55.

14. "Stephen Crane in Mexico," *Works*, vol. 8, 446–56.

15. *Works*, vol. 5, 13.

16. Crane to Nellie Crouse, 31 December [1895], Letter 122, *Letters*, 86.

17. Crane to Copeland and Day, 8 June 1895, Letter 72, *Letters*, 58.

18. Harry Thurston Peck, "Stephen Crane: Author of *The Black Riders, and Other Lines*," *Bookman* 1 (May 1895): 254.

19. *New York Tribune,* 9 June 1895, 24.

20. T. W. Higginson, "Recent Poetry," *Nation,* 24 October 1895, 296.

21. Crane to Willis Brooks Hawkins, 6, 10, and 18 September [1895], Letters 83, 84, 85, *Letters,* 63.

22. Crane to Ripley Hitchcock, 29 October [1895], Letter 91, *Letters,* 65.

23. *Harper's Weekly,* 26 Oct. 1895, 1013.

24. Crane to Willis Brooks Hawkins, 19 November [1895], Letter 108, *Letters,* 76.

25. Crane to Willis Brooks Hawkins, [ca. 12 November 1895], Letter 102, *Letters,* 72.

26. "Comment," *Lotus* 1 (1 March 1896) : 181.

27. *Bookman* 2 (February 1896) : 468.

28. Crane to Willis Brooks Hawkins, [ca. 6 or 7 November 1895] and [ca. 15 November 1895], Letters 98, 104, *Letters,* 70, 74.

29. Crane to Curtis Brown, 31 December 1896 [for 1895], Letter 123, *Letters,* 87.

30. Crane to Ripley Hitchcock, 27 January [1896], Letter 133, *Letters,* 106.

31. H. G. Wells, "Stephen Crane from an English Standpoint," *North American Review* 171 (August 1900) : 234.

32. Crane to Nellie Crouse, 5 February [1896], Letter 139, *Letters,* 111.

33. Ibid., 12 January 1896, Letter 129, *Letters,* 100.

34. Crane to S. S. McClure, 27 and 28 January [1896], Letters 135, 136, *Letters,* 107, 108.

35. Crane to Willis Brooks Hawkins, 27 January [1896], Letter 134, *Letters,* 107.

36. Crane to Ripley Hitchcock, 27 January [1896], Letter 133, *Letters,* 106.

37. Crane to William Dean Howells, 27 January [1896], Letter 132, *Letters,* 106.

38. Crane to Nellie Crouse, 26 January [1896], Letter 131, *Letters,* 105.

39. Crane to John Northern Hilliard, [ca. January 1896], Letter 137, *Letters,* 110.

40. Crane to the editor of *The Critic,* 15 February 1896, Letter 146, *Letters,* 117.

41. Crane to Nellie Crouse, 5 February [1896], Letter 139, *Letters,* 111.

42. Crane to Ripley Hitchcock, 26 and 30 March [1896], Letters 153, 154, *Letters,* 121–22.

43. Crane to Nellie Crouse, 1 and 18 March [1896], Letter 151, *Letters,* 120. Crane used the metaphor in a poem, "Oh, a rare old wine ye brewed for me/Flagons of despair. . . ." See *Works,* vol. 10, 81.

44. "Asbury Park as Seen by Stephen Crane," *Works,* vol. 8, 654.

45. *New York Journal,* 17 Sept. 1896; reprinted in *The New York City Sketches of Stephen Crane and Related Pieces,* ed. R. W. Stallman and E. R. Hagemann (New York: New York University Press, 1966), 222.

46. Frederic M. Lawrence to Thomas Beer, 8 November 1923, Letter 21, app., *Letters,* 332.

FIVE: FLORIDA AND GREECE

1. E. W. McCready to B. J. R. Stolper, 22 January 1934, Letter 25, app., *Letters*, 340.
2. "Stephen Crane's Own Story," *New York Press*, 7 Jan. 1897, 1–2. Also in *Works*, vol. 9, 89, 93–94.
3. Lillian Gilkes, *Cora Crane: A Biography* (Bloomington: Indiana University Press, 1960), 62.
4. *New York Press*, 4 Jan. 1897, 1–2.
5. *Works*, vol. 5, 68–92.
6. Ibid., 70, 76.
7. Ibid., 88.
8. Crane to William Howe Crane, 11 March 1897, *Stephen Crane Newsletter*, [I], No. 2 (Winter 1966) : 8.
9. Beer, 147.
10. Corwin Knapp Linson to Thomas Beer, 30 April 1923, Letter 19, app., *Letters*, 326.
11. Quoted by Scott C. Osborn in "Stephen Crane and Cora Taylor: Some Corrections," *American Literature* 26 (1954) : 417.
12. "An Impression of the Concert," *Westminster Gazette*, 3 May 1897, 1–2. Also in *Works*, vol. 9, 5–6.
13. Richard M. Weatherford, "A New Stephen Crane Letter," *American Literature* 48 (1976) : 80.
14. "The Man in the White Hat," *Westminster Gazette*, 18 June 1897, 1–2. Also in *Works*, vol. 9, 70, 72.
15. Quoted by Osborn, 417.
16. John Bass, "How Novelist Crane Acts on the Battlefield," *New York Journal*, 23 May 1892, 37; reprinted in *The War Dispatches of Stephen Crane*, ed. R. W. Stallman and E. R. Hagemann (New York: New York University Press, 1966), 42.
17. "A Fragment of Velestino," *Westminster Gazette*, 8 June 1897, Pt. III, 1–2. Also in *Works*, vol. 9, 40.
18. "Crane at Velestino," *New York Journal*, 11 May 1897, 1–2. Also in *Works*, vol. 9, 26.
19. *Works*, vol. 5, 139, 141.
20. Quoted by Beer, 153.

SIX: ENGLAND AND CUBA

1. Gilkes, 130.
2. Crane to John Northern Hilliard, [early Fall 1897?], Letter 216, *Letters*, 159.
3. Crane to James Gibbons Huneker, [ca. December 1897], Letter 217, *Letters*, 160.

4. Crane to William Crane, 29 October [1897], Letter 201, *Letters*, 147.

5. Ford Madox Ford, *Thus to Revisit* (London: Chapman and Hall, 1921), 107–8.

6. *Works*, vol. 8, 686–88.

7. "Adventures of a Novelist," *New Jork Journal*, 20 Sept. 1896, 17. Also in *Works*, vol. 8, 658.

8. *Works*, vol. 7, 24.

9. *Works*, vol. 5, 116–17.

10. Ibid., 120.

11. *Works*, vol. 5, 168–69.

12. Ibid., 165–66.

13. Crane to Paul Revere Reynolds, [October 1897], Letter 200, *Letters*, 145.

14. Ibid., [December 1897], Letter 214, *Letters*, 157.

15. Joseph Conrad, *Last Essays* (New York: Doubleday, 1926), 118.

16. Joseph Conrad, Introduction to *Stephen Crane*, by Thomas Beer (New York: Knopf, 1927), 4.

17. Ibid., 6.

18. Ibid., 16–17.

19. Joseph Conrad to Stephen Crane, 1 December 1897, Letter 210, *Letters*, 154.

20. Joseph Conrad to Edward Garnett, 5 December 1897, Letter 213, *Letters*, 156.

21. Beer, 165.

22. Conrad, Introduction to Beer, *Stephen Crane*, 32–33.

23. Crane to Sanford Bennett, [April 1898], Letter 231, *Letters*, 179.

24. "The Terrible Captain of the Captured Panama," *Works*, vol. 9, 103.

25. *Spectator*, 23 July 1898, 121.

26. Quoted by J. C. Levenson, Introduction to *Works*, vol. 5, cv–cvi, from typed copies of letters in Syracuse University Library.

27. Quoted by Scott C. Osborn, "The 'Rivalry-Chivalry' of Richard Harding Davis and Stephen Crane," *American Literature* 28 (March 1956): 55, from unpublished letter to family.

28. Quoted by Franklin Walker in *Frank Norris* (Garden City, New York: Doubleday, Doran, 1932), 176–77.

29. Ralph D. Paine, *Roads of Adventure* (Boston and New York: Houghton Mifflin, 1922), 243.

30. "War Memories," *Anglo-Saxon Review* 10 (December 1899): 10–38. Also in *Works*, vol. 6, 226–27.

31. *New York World*, 1 July 1898, 3. Also in *Works*, vol. 9, 134–42.

32. *Works*, vol. 10, 139.

33. Richard Harding Davis, *Notes of a War Correspondent* (New York: Scribner's, 1910), 125.

34. "War Memories," *Works*, vol. 6, 247.

35. Ibid., 254.

36. Don Carlos Seitz, "Stephen Crane: War Correspondent," *Bookman* **76** (February 1933): 139–40.

37. Crane to Paul Revere Reynolds, 27 September [1898], Letter 243, *Letters*, 187.

38. Quoted by J. C. Levenson, Introduction to *Works*, vol. 7, xxxvii, from letter of 24 October [1898], typed copy in Syracuse University Library.

39. Quoted by J. C. Levenson, Introduction to *Works*, vol. 5, cx, n., from letter of 1 November [1898], typed copy in Syracuse University Library.

40. Crane to Mrs. William Sonntag, 28 November 1898, Letter 255, *Letters*, 196.

41. Louis C. Senger to Hamlin Garland, 9 October 1900, Letter 12, app., *Letters*, 319.

42. Quoted by Beer, 207.

SEVEN: BREDE

1. Edward Garnett, "Mr. Stephen Crane: An Appreciation," *Academy*, **17** December 1898, 483–84.

2. Crane to Paul Revere Reynolds, 20 October [1898], Letter 247, *Letters*, 189.

3. Ford, 113.

4. Mark Barr, "Stephen Crane's Memorial," *New York Herald Tribune*, 2 Jan., 1940, Sec. 11, p. 9.

5. Ford, 111, 113.

6. Cora Crane to Edward Garnett, [January 1899], Letter 261, *Letters*, 203.

7. Crane to Mrs. Moreton Frewen, 15 May 1899, in J. C. Levenson, Introduction to *Works*, vol. 3, lxi.

8. Crane to James B. Pinker, [after 4 August 1899], Letter 277, *Letters*, 214.

9. Crane to James B. Pinker, [after 4 August 1899], Letters 272, 274, *Letters*, 211, 212.

10. James B. Pinker to Stephen Crane, 24 October 1899, Letter 309, *Letters*, 236.

11. *Works*, vol. 5, 171.

12. Quoted by R. W. Stallman, *Stephen Crane: A Biography* (New York: Braziller, 1968), 499.

13. Beer, 218–19.

14. Ford Madox Ford, *Portraits from Life* (Boston and New York: Houghton Mifflin, 1937), 30.

15. Conrad, Introduction to Beer, 25–26.

16. Ibid., 13–14.

17. Berryman, 244–45.

18. Beer, 233.

19. H. G. Wells, *Experiment in Autobiography* (New York: Macmillan, 1934), 524.

20. *Works*, vol. 6, 299, 300.
21. Crane to James B. Pinker, 4 November 1899, Letter 311, *Letters*, 238–39.
22. Crane to H. B. Marriott-Watson, 15 November 1899, Letter 315, *Letters*, 243.
23. Wells, *Experiment in Autobiography*, 522, 524.
24. Cora Crane to James B. Pinker, [2 January 1900], Letter 321, *Letters*, 257.
25. James B. Pinker to Cora Crane, 9 January 1900, Letter 327, *Letters*, 260. Pinker quotes from Crane's letter of 5 January, which has been lost.
26. Crane to James B. Pinker, 9 January [1900], Letter 328, *Letters*, 261.
27. Quoted by Berryman, 248.
28. Crane to Sanford Bennett, [14 May 1900], Letter 363, *Letters*, 283–84.
29. Quoted by Gilkes, 257.
30. "Funeral of Stephen Crane," *New York Tribune*, 29 June 1900, 8.

BIBLIOGRAPHY

WORKS BY STEPHEN CRANE

Maggie: A Girl of the Streets. [Johnston Smith, pseud.] New York: Privately printed, 1893. Revised edition (as Stephen Crane) New York: Appleton, 1896; London: Heinemann, 1896.

The Black Riders. Boston: Copeland and Day, 1895; London: Heinemann, 1896.

The Red Badge of Courage. New York: Appleton, 1895; London: Heinemann, 1896.

George's Mother. New York and London: Edward Arnold, 1896.

The Little Regiment. New York: Appleton, 1896; London: Heinemann, 1897.

The Third Violet. New York: Appleton, 1897; London: Heinemann, 1897.

The Open Boat. New York: Doubleday & McClure, 1898; London: Heinemann, 1898.

War Is Kind. New York: Stokes, 1899.

Active Service. New York: Stokes, 1899; London: Heinemann, 1899.

The Monster. New York and London: Harper, 1899. Enlarged edition, London and New York: Harper, 1901.

Whilomville Stories. New York and London: Harper, 1900.

Wounds in the Rain. New York: Stokes, 1900; London: Methuen, 1900.

Great Battles of the World. Philadelphia: Lippincott, 1901; London: Chapman & Hall, 1901.

Last Words. London: Digby, Long, 1902.

The O'Ruddy, by Crane and Robert Barr. New York: Stokes, 1903; London: Methuen, 1904.

The Sullivan County Sketches of Stephen Crane. Edited by Melvin Schoberlin. Syracuse, N.Y.: Syracuse University Press, 1949.

Stephen Crane: Uncollected Writings. Edited by O. W. Fryckstedt. Uppsala: Almqvist and Wiksell, 1963.

The War Dispatches of Stephen Crane. Edited by R. W. Stallman and E. R. Hagemann. New York: New York University Press, 1964.

The New York City Sketches of Stephen Crane. Edited by Stallman and Hagemann. New York: New York University Press, 1966.

Sullivan County Tales and Sketches. Edited by Stallman. Ames: Iowa State University Press, 1968.

The Notebook of Stephen Crane. Edited by Donald and Ellen Greiner. Charlottesville, Va.: A John Cook Wyllie Memorial Publication, 1969.

Stephen Crane in the West and Mexico. Edited by Joseph Katz. Kent, Ohio: Kent State University Press, 1970.

The Red Badge of Courage: A Facsimile Edition of the Manuscript. 2 vols. Edited by Fredson Bowers. Washington, D.C.: Bruccoli Clark/NCR Microcard Editions, 1973.

COLLECTIONS

The Work of Stephen Crane, 12 vols. Edited by Wilson Follett. New York: Knopf, 1925–1927.

The Collected Poems of Stephen Crane. Edited by Follett. New York and London: Knopf, 1930.

The Poems of Stephen Crane. Edited by Katz. New York: Cooper Square, 1966.

The Works of Stephen Crane. 10 vols. Edited by Fredson Bowers. Charlottesville: University Press of Virginia, 1969–1976.

LETTERS

Stephen Crane's Love Letters to Nellie Crouse. Edited by Edwin H. Cady and Lester G. Wells. Syracuse, N.Y.: Syracuse University Press, 1954.

Stephen Crane: Letters. Edited by R. W. Stallman and Lillian Gilkes. New York: New York University Press, 1960.

BIOGRAPHIES

Thomas Beer. *Stephen Crane: A Study in American Letters*. New York: Knopf, 1923.

John Berryman. *Stephen Crane*. New York: Sloane, 1950.

R. W. Stallman. *Stephen Crane: A Biography*. New York: Braziller, 1968.

REFERENCES

Frank Bergon. *Stephen Crane's Artistry*. New York and London: Columbia University Press, 1975.

Edwin H. Cady. *Stephen Crane*. Boston: Twayne, 1980.

Jean Cazemajou. *Stephen Crane: Écrivain Journaliste*. Paris: Librairie Didier, 1969.

Andrew Crosland. *A Concordance to the Complete Poetry of Stephen Crane*. Detroit: Gale Research/Bruccoli Clark, 1975.

Lillian Gilkes. *Cora Crane*. Bloomington: Indiana University Press, 1960.

Daniel Hoffman. *The Poetry of Stephen Crane*. New York: Columbia University Press, 1957.

Milne Holton. *Cylinder of Vision: The Fiction and Journalistic Writing of Stephen Crane*. Baton Rouge: Louisiana State University Press, 1972.

Marston LaFrance. *A Reading of Stephen Crane*. New York: Oxford University Press, 1971.

James Nagel. *Stephen Crane and Literary Impressionism*. University Park and London: Pennsylvania State University Press, 1980.

Eric Solomon. *Stephen Crane: From Parody to Realism*. Cambridge, Mass.: Harvard University Press, 1966.

————, *Stephen Crane in England: A Portrait of the Artist*. Columbus: Ohio State University Press, 1964.

Stephen Crane in Transition: Centenary Essays. Edited by Joseph Katz. Dekalb: Northern Illinois University Press, 1972.

Stephen Crane's Career: Perspectives and Evaluations. Edited by Thomas A. Gullason. New York: New York University Press, 1972.

BIBLIOGRAPHIES

Joan H. Baum. *Stephen Crane*. New York: Columbia University Libraries, 1956.

Matthew J. Bruccoli. *Stephen Crane 1871–1971*. Columbia: Department of English, University of South Carolina, 1971.

R. W. Stallman. *Stephen Crane: A Critical Bibliography*. Ames: Iowa State University Press, 1972.

INDEX